Master
the
Brand
Called
YOU™®

ASIA WOMEN'S NETWORK

We DREAM   We BELIEVE   We ACHIEVE

Here's to YOU™!

March 20-22, 2018

BRENDA BENCE

www.BrendaBence.com

Also by Brenda Bence

Would YOU Want to Work for YOU™?
How to Build an Executive Leadership Brand that
Inspires Loyalty and Drives Employee Performance

What's Holding YOU™ Back?
15 Executive Leadership Brand Behaviors
That Can Make or Break Your Career

Smarter Branding Without Breaking The Bank
Five Proven Marketing Strategies You Can Use Right Now to
Build Your Business at Little or No Cost

How YOU™ Are Like Shampoo
The Breakthrough Personal Branding System Based On
Proven Big-Brand Marketing Methods to Help You
Earn More, Do More, and Be More at Work

How YOU™ Are Like Shampoo for Job Seekers
The Proven Personal Branding System to Help You Succeed
in Any Interview and Secure the Job of Your Dreams

How YOU™ Are Like Shampoo for College Graduates
The Complete Personal Branding System to Define, Position,
and Market Yourself and Land a Job You Love

Branding Matters
How to Achieve Greater Success Through Powerhouse Branding
… For You, Your Products, and Your Company

Praise from around the world for

Master the Brand Called YOU™
by Brenda Bence

"This is the only book I've seen that provides you with a foolproof process for defining and establishing your personal brand in the workplace. Bence's personal branding system takes you from where you are now to where you want to be. Finally, someone has made personal branding simple!"

> — Thomas White, Group Head of Human Resources
> Zurich Insurance Group

"I have always thought Branding is about focusing on the *essence* of a thing — whether for a product, a company, or a country — and then communicating it in a way that truly understands the point of view of the receiver so that what you have to say is relevant and attractive to them. If I have been even partly right all these years, why wouldn't that apply to YOU — or should I say YOU™ — as a person, too? It is such a simple yet powerful idea. I wish I had thought of it!"

> — Tim Isaac, Vice Chairman-Asia Pacific
> Ogilvy & Mather

"Today's competitive marketplace requires that everyone find their niche — that goes for people, as well as products. The only way to achieve success is to build a trusted relationship that is remembered, and branding is how we stay in the minds of our audience. This book teaches people how to do just that in an extraordinarily friendly and no-nonsense way."

> — Julia Tuthill Mulligan, Managing Director
> Global New Ventures, Wm. Wrigley Jr. Company

"As a corporate marketer, Brenda Bence has built successful corporate brands all around the world. Now, she shows you how to make your own personal brand just as successful. Her straightforward approach to personal branding will ensure you stand out from the crowd, no matter what environment you are competing in."

> — Michael Wood, CEO-Greater China
> Leo Burnett Worldwide

"I have constantly found that the most effective candidates we interview have a clear definition of who they are, what they want (in both life and career), and where they need to go. Those who craft and communicate their personal brands achieve greater success not only when changing jobs or careers, but importantly when they take on new roles and responsibilities in their current organizations. The powerful personal branding system shared in this book allows the reader to do just that — achieve success through personal branding. Highly recommended!"

— Charles Moore, Managing Partner
Heidrick & Struggles

"Just like the process Brenda follows with her coaching clients, the easy steps outlined in this book present the reader with an amazing system to help you define, communicate, and take control of your career and your life. Reading through this book is like having Brenda sitting across the table from you, guiding you toward defining your brand and then toward mastering the everyday activities you do to help you live out your brand in pursuit of your dreams. Brenda will empower you to trust and respect yourself, and infect your world and others with your own unique 'shampoo,' assuring long-term success."

— Josephine Thompson, Master Certified Coach,
International Coach Federation, Accelerated Excellence

"If you are looking for a way to get ahead in your organization, this book will give you a blueprint for positively positioning yourself. Not only will Bence's book help you pinpoint and define your unique personal brand but it will also help you take charge of communicating it effectively, resulting in greater job and career success."

— Joyce L. Gioia, CMC, CSP, Strategic Business Futurist
Author of *How to Become an Employer of Choice*

"Now you can capitalize on the way big business goes about creating winning brands to brand yourself as a winner. In this book, Brenda Bence not only shares her big brand experience and skills as a strategic marketer, but also her talents as a successful coach. This book will help YOU create your unique brand. Read it now! It will make a difference in achieving your best, professionally and personally. Apply the lessons and grow, and have fun at the same time."

— Richard Czerniawski, President and Founder
Business Development Network International, Inc.

"Insightful and wise, this book is a definitive guide to achieving career success. Bence takes the mystery out of personal branding and brings it into the real world. This book is a great gift to anyone who wants to reach their full potential."

— Debra Fine, professional speaker and author of
The Fine Art of Small Talk and *The Fine Art of the Big Talk*

"Brenda has taken the same principles used for years to build hugely successful brands and made it possible for anybody to create an equally successful personal brand in the workplace. This should be required reading for everyone in business today whether they are working at a Fortune 500 or Inc 500 Company!"

— Paige Arnof-Fenn, Founder and CEO
Mavens & Moguls

"In this book, Bence takes personal branding to an entirely new level. Using the masterful strategies of corporate branders, she shows you step-by-step how to create a personal brand that can bring you more money, more recognition, a better position, or a better career. Highly recommended reading!"

— Steven W. Green, Vice President-Policy, Government,
and Public Affairs, Chevron Corporation

"If you follow the steps in this book, you will definitely stand out from the crowd. The great insights and steps provided help you define and successfully communicate your personal brand that, in a corporate environment, is critical for success."

— Doug Rath, Chairman
Talent Plus

"Brenda Bence provides you with the theory and practical application for establishing the most important brand, *your own*. Her professional, thoughtful approach is very engaging and, as you read, study, and implement her ideas, you will no doubt enhance your career and your life. She is a branding expert who makes it fun to follow her advice as you establish your own brand."

— Blaine Rieke, Retired Chairman and CEO
First Wisconsin Trust Company (now U.S. Bank)

"Having worked with branding principles for many years as an advertising executive, I've never seen them brought together in a personal branding system of this kind. One that is so clear and yet so comprehensive. When you read this book, you will see how you can use the same branding strategies that marketers use to create corporate brands, but on yourself. In doing so, you will create your own powerful personal brand that will help enhance you as a person ... and impact how other people see you."

— Dr. Sue Godfrey, Regional Director-Asia Pacific
Saatchi & Saatchi Ideas Company

Master
the
Brand
Called
YOU™®

The proven leadership personal
branding system to help you earn more,
do more, and be more at work

Brenda Bence

SENIOR EXECUTIVE COACH AND INTERNATIONAL BRANDING EXPERT

Published by Global Insight Communications LLC, Las Vegas, Nevada, U.S.A.

ISBN: 978-0-9825353-7-0
Library of Congress Control Number: 2014937748

Cover design by George Foster, Foster Covers (www.fostercovers.com)
Interior design and typesetting by Eric Myhr
Illustrations by Brenda Brown (webtoon.com)
Editing by Melanie Votaw (www.RidetheWord.com)

The stories in this book are based on real events and real people. Where requested, and in order to protect the privacy of certain individuals, names and identifying details have been changed.

Publisher's Cataloging-in-Publication data

Bence, Brenda S.

   Master the brand called you : the proven leadership personal branding system to help you earn more, do more, and be more at work / Brenda Bence.

   p. cm.
   ISBN 978-0-9825353-7-0

1. Success in business. 2. Branding (Marketing). 3. Leadership. 4. Brand choice. 5. Career development. I. Title.

HD69.B7 B38 2014
658.82720--dc23   2014937748

To Daniel
(The brand I am most loyal to)

My North
My South
My East
*My West**

* I get lost easily

Contents

Step 3: Avoid Damaging It

The Proven Pathway to Branding YOU™

Define it	Communicate it	Avoid Damaging it

Step 1

1 Audience
2 Need
3 Comparison

Outside

4 Strengths
5 Why
6 Character

Inside

Step 2

Leadership Personal Brand Marketing Plan

Short Summary:

Leadership Personal Brand Positioning

Actions
Reactions
Look
Sounds
Thoughts

Step 3

Leadership Personal Brand Busters®

YOU™

1

Do You Need a Leadership Personal Brand?

I always worry about people who say, "I'm going to do this for ten years [but] I really don't like it very well. And then I'll do this..." That's a little like saving up sex for your old age.

— Warren Buffett, Chairman of Berkshire Hathaway and the "Oracle of Omaha"

I have had the wonderful fortune of living in, working in, and visiting more than 80 countries, and as a result, I've met thousands of people from various walks of life all around the globe. And there's one thing that I have come to know as the truth: **We are all fundamentally the same.** We all ultimately want the same things: to earn a good living, enjoy our work, stay healthy, have a happy family life, enjoy meaningful friendships, and ultimately make a difference in some way.

So, if we're all the same, why would I write a book about leadership *personal* branding? Because while we are all fundamentally the same, we also each have specific gifts and talents that are as unique to us as our individual DNA. It's a bit of a paradox: We're the same and yet we're unique. And it's up to each of us to learn how to use our specific gifts and talents to make our lives and careers the best they can be—to make that difference in the world that we hope for. I also believe that it's up to each of us to learn *self*-leadership before we even begin to think about effectively leading others. This is where leadership personal branding comes in.

You've heard of serial killers? Well, think of me as a "serial brander"—I just can't stop branding! As a corporate marketer, I have worked for Procter & Gamble and Bristol-Myers Squibb on four different continents, where I was fortunate enough to manage many well-known brands like Pantene, Head & Shoulders, Vidal Sassoon, Ariel, Cheer, and Enfamil. I spent years defining, launching, and building brands all around the world using a definitive process and framework that corporate marketers have used for years to craft and communicate brands.

You may not have known that such a process exists, but trust me: Great brands don't get to be great by accident! It's only because of the process put in place by good, strategic marketers that these brands make millions. And it's only because of this process that successful brands not only survive but thrive through economic ups and downs.

You Aren't a Product Brand, But...

Several years ago, when I began actively coaching individuals to reach their goals and develop their own brands, I started to experiment with applying these same principles of corporate branding to people. I took the elements and framework used by corporate marketers and adjusted them to work for self-branding, so that we—as individuals—could thrive in our careers the same way successful name brands have thrived in the marketplace. Over time, I perfected this approach until it evolved into the unique leadership personal branding system I am sharing in this book—a system that walks you step by step through the process of building your own brand as a leader, whether you are focused on leading yourself or leading others. This is how you craft and effectively communicate YOU™®.[1] That's right—the trademarked YOU.

Today, you—or YOU™—can apply the same system in your work life that corporate marketers have used for years to build wildly successful product brands. Just as a corporate marketer uses this proven process to build mega-brands like Pantene, Apple, or Evian, you, too, can build the brand of YOU™.

Bring New Energy to Your Job

We all want to earn a good living and enjoy our work, but statistics indicate that few of us do. In fact, research shows that about 75% of

---

1. YOU™® is a registered trademark of Brand Development Associates (BDA) International, Ltd.

employees today are unhappy with their jobs. Can you imagine this? We spend more than half of our waking hours at work, yet 75% of us are unhappy while we're there!

If you're one of those people who aren't as satisfied at work as you'd like to be, defining your own leadership brand can help you start to enjoy your job again. Once you define and clarify your role at work and what you want to accomplish—which is what leadership personal branding is all about—your work will have new meaning. Knowing who YOU™ are can help you eliminate that groan that escapes from your throat when the alarm goes off in the morning. Yes, you *can* be happy, fulfilled, and motivated on the job.

When you look at your work as an opportunity to build a brand for yourself, you start to make every minute of your career count. It brings new energy and purpose to your job. When people ask you what you do, you'll be able to answer the question with enthusiasm.

Grab the Steering Wheel of Your Career

Author and motivational speaker Nido Qubein said, "Life doesn't give you what you want; it gives you what you deserve." What you focus on is what you get. So, if you want a better career and a more satisfying work life, it's up to you. Your success at work is in your control, and a large part of the foundation of that control comes from learning how to master the brand called YOU™.

Defining your brand is only the first step in the process, though. It makes no sense to get clear on the brand you want and then leave it in a desk drawer. In order for your brand to serve you well, you need a roadmap to help you *communicate to others* what you want it to stand for. That's how you achieve your goals. That's how you change your work life for the better. That's how you master self-leadership and become a leader of others, if that's what you want in your career. And that's how you grab the steering wheel of your career and drive it to where you want it to go.

Believe It or Not...You Already Have a Brand as a Leader

When I speak about leadership personal branding at conventions and corporate gatherings, often an audience member will say, "Sounds very interesting, Brenda, but no thanks. I'm actually not into *self-promotion*, and I'm not a leader. I don't have—or even want—a leadership personal brand."

It's then that I break the news: **You already have one.**

It's true. You don't have to sit down and give your brand any thought to have one. Just by virtue of being you in the workplace, you are branded. And whether or not you lead others, you *do* lead yourself. The question is: Do you have the leadership personal brand you want?

If you don't take control of your leadership personal brand and make a conscious decision about how you want to be known, you may be leaving an impression that actually works *against* your success. Are you living up to the potential that YOU™ could achieve if you took charge of your brand consciously rather than leaving it to chance?

Don't Like the Brand You Have Now? Change It.

Many years ago, a famous man discovered the hard way that his leadership personal brand wasn't what he wanted it to be. Alfred Nobel was a very successful and wealthy Swedish industrialist who lived in the 1800s. He was widely credited with two inventions—dynamite and the detonator (the apparatus that causes dynamite to ignite from a distance). He had made millions from these two inventions, and he was living a wonderful millionaire's life.

Alfred's brother, Ludwig Nobel, was an equally well-known and wealthy businessman who had developed successful inventions of his own. You might say that Alfred and Ludwig Nobel were the Bill Gates and Steve Jobs of their day.

In April of 1888, Ludwig Nobel died. But the death notice that showed up the next day in the newspaper was switched, and it was *Alfred's* obituary that appeared, not Ludwig's. So, Alfred Nobel had the rare opportunity of opening up the morning paper and reading his own death notice. Can you imagine how powerful that would be?

But Alfred must have cringed when he read the headline of his obituary. It labeled him "The Merchant of Death" because of all of the work that he had done with dynamite and detonators. In that single moment, Alfred Nobel realized that everything he had done would forever associate his name with death—unless he took control and did something about it.

That was the day the seed was planted for the Nobel Prizes. Alfred didn't want the name "Nobel" to stand for death and destruction, so he made a plan to develop a series of prizes for those who confer "the greatest benefit on mankind." When he died, he left the bulk of his millions to the establishment of the awards that eventually included five categories: Physics, Chemistry, Physiology/Medicine, Literature, and Peace.

Look at what the name "Nobel" stands for today—the most prestigious prizes awarded for the highest achievements of humankind. While you've no doubt heard of the Nobel Prizes, you might not have known about the other work that Alfred Nobel did in his life. This is a true testament to the fact that he was successful in changing his brand so that his name could stand for what he wanted.

The same holds true for you. If you aren't happy with the brand you have now, you can change it. As author Carl Bard said, "Though no one can go back and make a brand-new start, anyone can start from now and make a brand-new ending." This book can help you kick start that brand new beginning.

A "Systematic" Way to Master Your Brand

Now that you know you already have a brand, it's time to take control of it by learning how to manage it. Since the advent of personal branding, several books have been written on the subject. What I have tried to do with *Master the Brand Called YOU™* is to offer you a **complete system** that covers every possible aspect of building a leadership personal brand for yourself. This book goes beyond the theory of personal branding to bring you tangible applications for your brand within your day-to-day work life. It's a do-it-yourself, no-nonsense guide to achieving greater success at work through branding yourself. It's simple, easy to read, and has worked for thousands around the world.

Master the Brand Called YOU™ is designed to take the guesswork out of figuring out what your brand is and how to make it work for you. Through this proven step-by-step system, you will:

- Define your own brand using a Leadership Personal Brand Positioning Statement format, which is modeled off the six core positioning elements used by the most successful product brands in the world.

- Communicate your leadership personal brand through a Leadership Personal Brand Marketing Plan that will help you take charge of the five activities you do every day that most impact your brand.

- Avoid damaging your leadership personal brand by learning from the mistakes of others. This is one of the most unique and fun parts of the system—my Leadership Personal Brand Busters®. These will help you bypass the most common pitfalls to establishing your brand so that you'll know what to watch out for before you even get there.

- Use the graphic labeled "The Proven Pathway to Branding YOU™" on page 14 like a map to understand each step of this leadership personal branding system. Don't worry if it doesn't all make sense to you right now. It will—I promise.

I will also give you tangible tools to help you check the development of your leadership personal brand three months from now, six months from now, and further down the road. You will discover ways to assess your progress so that your brand will stay on track and evolve as your career moves forward.

As you read these pages, I hope you will experience many "ah-ha!" moments that stem from the power of thinking of yourself as a unique and individual brand. I hope you'll see how you can use leadership personal branding to make tangible changes in your career. Those changes can bring you the kind of success you have always wanted but weren't sure how to achieve, resulting in increased income, greater job satisfaction, and faster career progress.

Input Equals Output

Master the Brand Called YOU™ is an interactive, action-oriented experience, but your leadership personal brand won't be handed to you on a silver platter. I can guarantee you one thing for sure: What you put *in* to defining and communicating your brand as a leader is exactly what you will get *out* of it. The more time and energy you devote to this process, the faster and better your results will be.

Get ready to feel empowered as you take charge of your brand and become the Brand Manager of YOU™.

2

The Power of Brands

A brand is a living entity—and it is enriched or undermined cumulatively over time, the product of a thousand small gestures.

— Michael Eisner, former CEO of Disney

No book about leadership personal branding would be complete without an understanding of the powerful and influential role that brands play in our modern-day lives. *Time* magazine once reported that the average American citizen living in a large urban area runs across an estimated 3,000 brands every single day. When I first read that statistic, I couldn't believe it. But then, the proof was right in front of me when I would walk down Michigan Avenue in Chicago and look at all of the signs, or I would stand in Times Square in New York City and see brand after brand after brand.

In fact, I suspect that seeing 3,000 brands—which is almost certainly an even larger number today—holds true for anyone living and working in a large urban environment anywhere in the world. Ride in a taxi from downtown Bangkok out to the airport with hundreds of billboards lining the way, or walk down a supermarket aisle in London with the myriad of brands peering down at you.

Think about it. How many brands have *you* seen today on product labels, the side of a bus, the top of a taxi, or on the Internet? Everywhere you look, brand names are screaming for your attention. Brands are everywhere, and they are such a part of our day-to-day lives that we may not even think about them.

But out of those thousands of brands you encounter every day, if you're like most people, you will probably stay faithful to a handful of brands throughout most of your life. After all, great brands build intense loyalty. How about you? What brands are you loyal to? Would you consider it out of the question, for example, to buy anything but a Canon camera or to switch from using your Gillette shaving cream? Why? What is the allure of that favorite brand of yours? What does it offer you that no other brand can?

Brands can be extremely big and influential, too. Take Coca-Cola as an example. That one brand alone brings in an estimated $16 billion in sales every year, more than *$1 billion every single month*. As of this writing, that represents more than the Gross Domestic Product of 86 different countries. How's *that* for powerful?

The Untouchables

So, what do we know so far? We know that brands are everywhere, that they can create intense loyalty, and that they can be mighty big. Is there any question why I find brands so fascinating?

But what's even more amazing about brands is that they are all this … yet, you cannot touch them. You can smell the aroma of a Starbucks cup of coffee, you can taste the kick of a Mentos when you pop one in your mouth, you can hear the sound of Microsoft's Windows booting up, you can feel the wet aluminum of a cold can of Sprite in your hand, and you can see the golden arches of McDonald's logo. But you cannot *touch* a brand. The smell, touch, or sight of a product is really only a representation of that brand. The brand itself is actually intangible. Its power exists only in your mind.

Can these intangible "brands" truly influence the way we act and think? Let's explore.

Powerful Brand Images

Great brands are like people. They have a personality and a character all their own. To demonstrate what I mean, pause for a moment, look around you, and find two doorways that you can see from where you are. In the first doorway, imagine that Mercedes Benz—the brand—is standing there as a *person*. What kind of person would the Mercedes Benz brand be? Is it a man or a woman? What profession does this person have? What is this person wearing? What is the income level of this person—low, medium, or high? What is his or her favorite pastime?

Now, look at the second doorway, and imagine that Ferrari—the brand—is standing there as a person. What kind of person would the Ferrari brand be? Is it a man or a woman? What profession does this person have? How is this person dressed—more formally or more casually than Mercedes Benz? What is the income level of this person— higher or lower? What is his or her favorite pastime?

Compare the answers to both sets of questions. If you're like most people, your answers will be quite different. Even though Mercedes Benz and Ferrari are both high-end luxury cars that can get you from one place to another, the brand images of Mercedes Benz and Ferrari are not the same. That's because you *perceive, think,* and *feel* differently about these two brands. Those perceptions, thoughts, and feelings have been carefully created in your mind by smart marketers who understand the art and the science of branding.

That's right. Branding, whether of a product or a person, is both an art *and* a science. On the one hand, brands appeal to your logic—you *think* rationally about them—so, this is where the science comes in. But branding is also an art because brands appeal to your emotions—how you *feel* about them.

Consider This

Think for a moment about the brands that have earned your loyalty. Maybe you have even traveled out of your way to find and buy that special brand that's like no other. What if you could harness that same kind of power with your own individual brand as a leader? You can. Building your leadership brand at work can help you have that type of influence on the job.

Branding People?

I firmly believe that people—just like products—are brands, too. Let's use examples of people we probably all know—starting with celebrities. What do you perceive, think, and feel when you hear the name "Ashton Kutcher"? What do you perceive, think, and feel when you hear the name "Hugh Jackman"? Both of these actors are good-looking leading men, but they create very different perceptions, thoughts, and feelings, don't they? Now, let's throw "Jackie Chan" into the picture … you have different perceptions, thoughts, and feelings about him, too.

Think of any category of well-known people—how about singers this time. Consider Taylor Swift … Lady Gaga … Adele. Again, they're all very different. That's because each of these individuals has a very specific brand that is absolutely unique and ownable as compared to the others.

"But, wait a minute, Brenda," you may be saying. "These examples are celebrities, and they have the funds and the means to hire full-time image specialists to manage *their* personal brands!"

Fair point. But you don't need high-priced help to define and communicate your *leadership* personal brand. The system shared in *Master the Brand Called YOU™* will help you build your brand without writing checks to a publicist. It's designed for the millions of people all around the world who may not be famous and certainly don't plan on turning their individual brand into a global household name. What you want to do is define yourself in *your world* in order to achieve your personal career goals.

Leadership Personal Branding Is *Not* All About You

What is this concept called "leadership personal branding"? I like to define it as:

The way you want people to perceive,
think, and feel about you as a leader
in relation to other leaders.

Just like product brands such as Mercedes-Benz and Ferrari exist in our minds, so your own leadership personal brand exists in the minds of others, as they perceive, think, and feel about you in relation to other leaders at work.

Let's look carefully at this definition, and focus on three key words: perceive, think, and feel. They've been carefully chosen for a reason.

Perceive: Perception in branding is reality. When it comes to your own brand, it doesn't matter who *you* think you are. What matters is how *others* perceive you. If others perceive you differently from who you actually believe you are inside, you're probably not communicating the brand you want.

Think: On the one hand, branding is a fairly rational exercise, so our brains have a lot to do with how we think about brands. There are logical reasons why we choose one brand over another. The same holds true in leadership personal branding—what do others *think* about you?

Feel: On the other hand, branding is also an emotional process. Earlier in the chapter, you thought about brands that have earned your loyalty over the years. Stop and reflect on one of those brands right now. What is the *feeling* you have about that brand? Trust? Admiration? Gratitude? We establish connections with brands, and these connections go far beyond what the products actually do for us. We're loyal to these brands based on *emotional* connections—and it's the same with leadership personal branding. The way people feel about you has a profound influence on your success. The stronger the connections you create with others, the more powerful your individual brand will be.

Colleagues' Brands at Work

Still don't believe the average person has a brand? Think of someone in your current job who is enjoyable to be around—the kind of person you look forward to seeing and speaking with every morning. Stop for a moment and consider: How do you perceive this person? What do you think about this individual? How does he or she make you feel?

Now, consider a different person you work with who—let's be honest—you really *don't* enjoy working with all that much. It's that one person who seems to cause you problems and tie your stomach in knots. How do you perceive him or her? What do you think about this individual? How does *this* person make you feel?

Can you see how these two people have very different "brands"? And their brands have nothing to do with who *they* think they are. Their brands exist in *your* mind, based on how you perceive, think, and feel about them. And if they haven't taken the time to define their best possible leadership personal brands, they may be seriously limiting their success by presenting themselves in a way that is different from how they want to be seen.

The Experience of YOU™

As a brand *passionista*, I enjoy finding analogies between corporate brands and personal brands. With that in mind, here's a favorite that absolutely speaks to the importance of creating a powerful leadership personal brand. (See how long it takes you to figure out which corporate brand I'm describing.)

- If you had invested $10,000 in this company when it first went public in 1992, it would be worth more than $1,000,000 today.

- According to an article on *Forbes.com*, this brand currently has approximately 18,000 stores located in over 50 countries.

- If you haven't guessed it yet, this should help: Every morning, millions of people start their days by visiting one of this company's outlets for their favorite cup of java.

Yes, indeed, I'm talking about Starbucks.

Now, a lot (and I mean a *lot*) has been talked about, written about, and discussed about the Starbucks brand—and for good reason. Starbucks became the game-changer for the centuries-old, staid coffee industry.

But what can Starbucks' branding success teach you about your own brand? What follows is an analogy originally based on a *Brandweek* magazine article (with updated statistics to reflect today's prices):

- Coffee, when it is in its natural bean state, is a commodity that sells for about 3 to 5 cents per cup.

- Add packaging and a brand name to that coffee, place it on a grocery store shelf, and the price rises to 10 to 50 cents per cup.

- That same coffee offered up with service and a smile (say, at a Dunkin' Donuts) increases the price to about $1-$2 per cup.

- Then there's Starbucks, which sells its coffee worldwide for anywhere from $4 to $8 per cup. Imagine—people flock there by the millions to spend *four times more* for a cup of coffee than anywhere else.

How does Starbucks get us to spend so much more of our hard-earned cash—and feel good about it while we're doing it? Because it offers its consumers so much more than just a good cup of coffee; it provides a *rewarding coffee experience*. At Starbucks, we're paying for the pleasure of taking a break during the day—watching the skilled baristas concoct our favorite choca-locca-mocha-frocha (I can never get those names right) and enjoy a relaxing chat with friends after a night out.

That's what differentiates Starbucks from the dozens of other coffee brands out there and what has built such strong brand loyalty through the years, despite its higher price tag. So, what does this demonstrate?

People will pay more for a superior experience.

Applying this truth to your own brand as a leader means that if you want to earn more money, advance in your career, and rise to positions of greater responsibility, you must think about the *experience* you offer on the job. Think about it ... would you want to work with you? What would it be like to be your colleague, your peer, your boss, or your direct report? What would that *experience* be like? Again, it's all about the way key people perceive, think, and feel about YOU™.

Taking Control of YOU™

As I said earlier, you already have a leadership personal brand, even if you didn't think you needed or wanted one. Your brand may be out there doing its thing, creating perceptions about YOU™ without you even being aware of it. People may be thinking and feeling about you in ways that aren't at all how you want to be perceived, just like Alfred Nobel. Most people I've met find this idea intriguing ... and a little bit scary. They don't like the idea that their personal brands may be running amuck without knowing what to do about it.

The leadership personal branding system in this book will help you uncover and eliminate any disconnect between how others see your brand and how you *want* to be seen. Some of the questions you will answer as you move through the steps of the system are:

- How do you take control of your leadership brand if it exists in the minds of others?

- What can you do to make sure your brand as a leader is what you want it to be?

- How do you want others to perceive, think, and feel about you?

- How can you make your leadership personal brand something that is definable and that you own?

- How do you communicate your brand effectively?

Your Leadership Personal Brand Triangle™

Take a look at the Leadership Personal Brand Triangle™ in the graphic below. This is a concept I developed to help you understand how well your current brand is aligned with your desired brand.

Your *Desired* Leadership Personal Brand

| **Your Leadership Personal Brand As *You* See It Now** | | **Your Leadership Personal Brand As *Others* See It Now** |

For your brand to be strong, all of the descriptions at the three points of your triangle should be the same. How do you get a crystal clear and consistent grip on what those three points stand for right now? Do what I call "The Five Words Exercise":

Step 1. Sit down and ask yourself: "What five adjectives would I use to describe myself as a leader at work?" Don't overthink it, but do think in both positive and negative terms. An example might be: Strategic, hardworking, intelligent, team player, impatient. Write down your five words right now.

Step 2. Ask: "What five adjectives would I *like* others to use to describe me as a leader at work?" This is the foundation of your *desired* leadership personal brand. Write down those five words as well. How similar or different are they from the first set of words?

Step 3. Next, recruit someone you trust to be your "brand ambassador." Give that person the names of five to ten individuals to interview (people you work with). Have your ambassador ask those people individually to share the first five adjectives that come to mind when they hear your name. The ambassador should ask your feedback providers to keep their answers to specific words and not phrases; this helps ensure that the exercise outcomes are simple and easily analyzed. By the way, make sure the ambassador does not write down anyone's name or note who said what; anonymity is key to this exercise! For this approach to work, all information must be kept confidential.

Step 4. Once you receive the compiled list of words from all five to ten people, spend some time reviewing the list. What similarities or trends do you see? What adjectives are similar or different? When you see words repeated, you will know that they are part of your brand. When you see a variety of different words, it may indicate that you're acting one way with certain people and another way with others. Beware: This inconsistency can lead to leadership personal brand confusion.

Once you work through the entire *Master the Brand Called YOU*™ personal branding system, you will be well on your way to aligning the three points of your Leadership Personal Brand Triangle. No matter how successful you already are, you will then have the opportunity to distinguish yourself further in the workplace.

Just as Starbucks can command a much higher price tag than a standard cup of coffee at a local cafe, so YOU™ can create a premium leadership personal brand that commands a bigger paycheck, better perks, and/or brings you greater recognition and satisfaction in your career.

Think of it this way: Your leadership personal brand is what you stand for in the minds of others. Who is _____™? Insert your name in the blank, and let's begin.

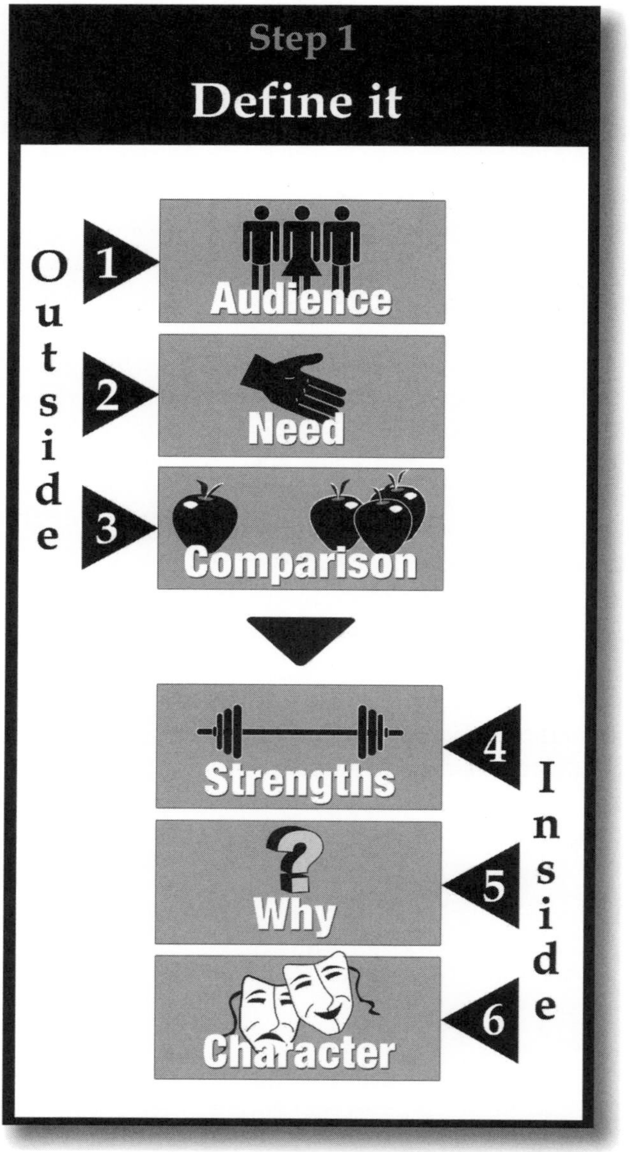
Step 1
Define it
Outside
1 Audience
2 Need
3 Comparison
4 Strengths
5 Why
6 Character
Inside

3

Defining Your
Leadership Personal Brand

*I always wanted to be somebody,
but I should have been more specific.*

— Lily Tomlin, actress and comedian

Now you know that you cannot *touch* your leadership personal brand because it exists in the minds of others. So, if you can't touch your brand, how can you control and master it? It may seem like an incredibly tough challenge, but product brands have been successfully created in the minds of millions of consumers for years and years, so you *can* absolutely take control of your brand as a leader as well. The key is to do what all successful product brands do as a first step—Define it.

Fact: Every brand that you know and love uses six positioning elements to carefully define that brand. It doesn't even matter if the marketers managing those brands are aware of these elements. Trust me—all six are a vital part of what makes every brand tick, and it's a tried-and-true formula.

You've already asked yourself the question, "Who is [insert your name here]—The Trademarked YOU™?" And you may be saying, "Honestly, I have no idea how to answer that question." If this is the case, don't worry. We will work with a specific formula that borrows from these six brand positioning elements and which is used by marketing experts around the world. That formula will help you pinpoint the best possible leadership personal brand for you at work.

The Power of a Framework

Let's take a look at the six elements of this formula as they apply to the product brands that we all love and use every day. Then, we'll explore how to apply those same elements to YOU™.

THE BRAND DEFINITION FRAMEWORK	
Product Brands	**Leadership Personal Brands**
Target: When it comes to name brand products, this is the "Target Market." Who will buy the product—men, women, college graduates, people with high incomes or low incomes? What are their hopes, dreams, and fears? What attitudes do they have toward the brand or the type of product in question? What can you learn about them by the way they act toward a particular brand?	*Audience:* Like a Target Market, your "Audience" consists of the people you want to influence with your leadership personal brand. Maybe your Audience is an individual, like your boss, or a group of people, like the division of your company. Or maybe it's an internal or external customer. Who do you want to impact with *your* brand?
Need: What does the Target Market *need*? When companies create a brand, they try to respond to a Need of their Target Market that hasn't yet been filled. Or maybe they aim at meeting a Need in a way that's better than competing brands.	*Need:* If your Audience is your boss, for example, what does he or she need? Is there a gap that hasn't been filled in the company? For example, your boss might need someone to take certain responsibilities off of his or her shoulders.

Product Brands	Leadership Personal Brands
Competitive Framework: When it comes to product brands, "competitive framework" is all about the brands that compete for your attention. Many brands are trying to get noticed, so what makes you choose one brand over another?	*Comparison:* In leadership personal branding, it's more about *comparing* than competing. Who will your Audience compare you to when it comes to fulfilling a Need they've identified?
Benefits: What specific offerings or promises does a product brand provide its customers? In the case of a toothpaste brand, it might be the ability to help prevent cavities in children so that consumers can feel like good parents.	*Unique Strengths:* In leadership personal branding, your Unique Strengths are the benefits that you bring to the table. Just like with product brands, your strengths are the specific promises you offer your Audience.
Reasons Why: Why should the Target Market believe a product brand can deliver what it says it can? These are a brand's "Reasons Why." They can be based on a number of brand aspects, like its ingredients, its experience in the marketplace, how the product is designed, or maybe a strong endorsement.	*Reasons Why:* Why should people believe YOU™ can deliver the Unique Strengths that you promise? Reasons Why help you prove you can do what you say you can.

Product Brands	Leadership Personal Brands
Brand Character: Think of this as the "personality" of a brand. What words would you use to describe a product brand if that brand were a person?	*Brand Character:* What is the Character of your own distinct brand? Think of this as a reflection of your personality, your overriding attitude, and your temperament. It's an important foundation of who YOU™ are.

I've divided the six elements in our leadership personal brand definition framework into two categories: those elements that come from **outside** ourselves and those elements that come from **inside**. In other words, the first three elements—Audience, Need, and Comparison—all relate to people or things that happen *outside* of you. The last three elements—Unique Strengths, Reasons Why, and Brand Character—all relate to things that happen *inside* of you. You can see this graphically via the Step 1 diagram on page 30.

Your Leadership Personal Brand Positioning Statement

As we work our way through Step 1—the "Define it" step—you'll be given the tools to complete a form called your "Leadership Personal Brand Positioning Statement," which is set up in a format using the six positioning elements from Step 1. Your Leadership Personal Brand Positioning Statement will show you exactly how to define who you really are. Bottom line: This is how "you" become "YOU™."

At the end of each upcoming chapter, you will be able to complete one more portion of your Positioning Statement, just like the one outlined here. The second half of the book will show you how to *communicate* and *avoid damaging* the brand you've worked so hard to create.

YOUR Leadership Personal Brand Positioning Statement

Audience

My Audience is:

Demographics ("Provable" social characteristics of this person, such as age, sex, income, education, etc.):

Psychographics (More psychologically-oriented personality traits of this individual, including attitudes, mindset, etc.):

Key Behaviors (Observable manners of behaving or acting):

Needs

My Audience's Needs are:

Functional:

Emotional:

Comparison

Job Title:

Desired Identity: I want to be the brand of *(the way I would like to be perceived):*

Unique Strengths

My Existing Unique Strengths are:

The Future Unique Strengths That I Want to Work on are:

Reasons Why

My Existing Reasons Why (why my Audience should believe I can deliver my Unique Strengths) *are:*

The Future Reasons Why That I Want to Work on are:

> ## Brand Character
>
> *My Leadership Personal Brand Character (how I want my Leadership Personal Brand Character to be perceived, including my overriding attitude, temperament, and personality)* **is:**

By the time you have finished working with the six-element formula and your Leadership Personal Brand Positioning Statement, you'll be ready to put YOU™ into action. Roll up your sleeves! Your leadership personal brand is waiting...

Define it

O
u
t
s
i
d
e

1 ▶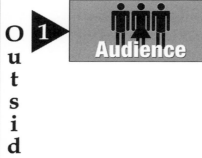

Step 1

4

Leadership Personal Brand Positioning Element #1: *Audience*

It's up to the Audience. It always has been.
— Kate Smith, singer

Your leadership personal brand is all about how you want people to perceive, think, and feel about you as a leader, either as a self-leader or as a leader of others. But who are these people who are doing the perceiving, the thinking, and the feeling? They are your Audience.

Your "Audience" isn't necessarily sitting in a theatre or conference room while you give a performance or a presentation. Your Audience is actually anyone you want to influence with your leadership personal brand. It might be an individual, such as your boss, a colleague, or a customer. It might be a small group of people, such as the accounting department, the board of directors, or personnel who work at one of your suppliers. Your Audience could be a large group of people, such as your sales division or a network of people in your field. Or, it could indeed be a group of 1,000 people sitting in a hotel ballroom while you deliver a presentation.

In product branding, the Target Market (the equivalent to Audience) almost always includes "demographics." What does that mean? Demographics are *facts* about people—provable social characteristics, such as age, sex, income, education, etc. To a marketer, this is critical information, and brand managers regularly field demographic studies to understand their Target Market better. Whether the target is female or male, what age range, what income bracket they are in, whether the target lives in the city or the suburbs ... those are the kinds of facts that the standard marketer is after.

Unfortunately, a lot of marketers stop there and don't go any further. But demographics are only the *basics* of branding and marketing—the tip of the iceberg.

Think about it for a moment: If you really want to get to know someone, is it enough only to know his or her age, income bracket, and where he or she was born? It wouldn't really tell you much about that person. You would only have scratched the surface, and you would have to base all of your assumptions about that person on little more than what you could read in a census form.

That's why the best brand-builders take the time to go deeper. They want to know much more about their Target Market. They want to get into the heads of the people who are buying their brands and understand their behavior. In marketing, this has a name—"psychographics"—which basically means information about your Target Market that is based on *psychodynamics*. In short, psychographics are about what makes a Target Market tick.

The Audience for your leadership personal brand will be much smaller than the Target Market for the average product brand. This is the good news! But just like any great brand marketer, as a leadership personal brander, you need to get into the heads of your Audience. You, too, need to know what makes them tick. Where are they in their lives? What are their attitudes and behaviors? What do they value and care about? Where do they focus their energy?

This is fundamental because unless you know your Audience, you cannot possibly define a viable brand for yourself. Simply put, the better you know your Audience, the more successful your brand as a leader will be. This step is the foundation of your brand, and it's critical to get this part right so that the other steps which follow will flow well.

Who *Is* Your Audience Anyway?

Who are the one to three key people you believe make up the critical Audience for your leadership personal brand? Remember: These are the people who can most directly influence your career and those who you *most want to impact* with your brand.

Have a Large Audience? Try the "Audience of One"

What if the people who have the greatest impact on your career aren't *individuals* like your boss, the CEO, your customer, or a vendor? What if your Audience is a large group, like an entire division within your company or a cluster of customers? How can you possibly get to know the demographics, psychographics, and behaviors of every single person? Well, you can't, and fortunately, you don't have to.

Instead, use what I call an "Audience of One." Don't get overwhelmed by having a large group of people in your Audience; think of *one person* in that group who is the most representative in terms of demographics, psychographics, and behavior. Then, think of that individual as *the* person who represents that larger group.

For example, what if your Audience is the finance division of your company, and there are 60 people within that group? Do your best to choose one person who you believe best represents the majority of the people in that division. Let's say that most of the individuals in the finance division are in their mid-to-late 30s, married, and live in the suburbs of your city. They tend to be both family-oriented and politically progressive, active in the community, and hard-working. Write down all of the characteristics that you can pinpoint about the majority of the people in the division. Then, compare your list of characteristics with the names of the people who work in that division. Which individual could best represent the overall group? This person will become your Audience of One.

Of course, this doesn't mean that you'll communicate only with this one person. It just means that you'll use the information about this one person as a way of identifying and outlining the characteristics of your Audience. Using the Audience of One concept can work perfectly for your Leadership Personal Brand Positioning Statement, and it will make your job as a self-brander that much easier.

Consider This

When you change jobs or careers, you have a new Audience that you must learn about. Even if you stay in your current position, your Audience may change from time to time, such as when you get a new boss or add a new customer.

Do Your Have the Right Audience?

One leadership personal brand client of mine, Gavin, doesn't work in a corporate job. He's a professional speaker who presents regularly to large groups of corporate executives and employees. Gavin had become a very popular speaker in his native country of South Africa, evidenced by the fact that he was booked all the time. He was even asked to speak several years in a row by the same conventions and conferences where his unusual style was particularly loved. His approach was a bit on the "irreverent and naughty" side; he really loved to shake things up, and he had the ability to make his Audiences think differently. For example, while other professional speakers wore suits and ties, Gavin arrived on stage in shorts, a t-shirt, and a baseball cap. His baseball cap even became his symbol of sorts—his mascot for thinking outside of the box.

When Gavin decided he wanted to expand his brand and take it internationally, he first consulted with a group of professionals that he met with regularly for advice and encouragement. This group concluded that, outside of South Africa, Gavin would need to tone down his act. They didn't believe his "crazy behavior" would be well accepted in Europe or North America. Gavin assumed they were right, but this was difficult news to hear. How could he be true to himself if he tempered his mischievous personality? He felt that was the core of who he really was—his authentic self.

Around this time, Gavin attended a convention for the Global Speakers Federation (GSF) in Dubai, where he heard me speak on personal branding. Afterward, he came up to me, introduced himself, and said, "Help—my personal brand is broken!" I laughed, of course, and said, "No personal brand is *broken*! It's probably just in need of some direction. Let's talk."

Gavin and I worked together over a period of time to carefully define his brand, and we came to a key conclusion: His brand wasn't broken at all—in fact, his brand was thriving! He was well known and appreciated in South Africa because he had carved out a unique niche for himself that was ownable and exciting.

His leadership personal brand challenge wasn't to *change* what he was doing or how he was doing it. What Gavin needed to do was to be more specific about the *definition of his Audience*. He could maintain the same personal brand he had perfected over time, but he needed to define his Audience in a way that would allow him to quickly seek out and find just the right people who needed, liked, and desired his style. It was true that his brand of humor and irreverence wouldn't be right for some companies or certain managers, but for others, he would be considered a breath of fresh air.

This is what is called a "niche strategy" in marketing. Gavin didn't need to be all things to all people. He simply needed to identify and find just the right people who needed him and his message.

The moral of this story? If your leadership personal brand truly expresses who you are, don't change YOU™! Make sure you are targeting the right Audience for your unique brand, and don't change what's working. Define the type of Audience who will genuinely appreciate what you have to offer, and search out that Audience. In other words, always be true to "YOU™rself."

Get Personal!

In these days of e-mails, VOIP, Facebook, Twitter, Instagram, text messages, and YouTube, it can sometimes feel like we're losing our personal connections with each other. Getting to know your brand's Audience, however, requires a more direct personal connection. The world's best marketers build a link between the brand they manage and their Target Market. You should do the same with your Audience in order to effectively define and communicate your leadership personal brand.

You may be thinking, "But I'm not a mind reader... how can I get into my boss's head?" or "How can I find out that level of detail about a particular customer?" To thoroughly understand your Audience, you don't have to learn the art of telepathy, but you do have to *ask*. People love to talk about themselves and, while you don't want to leap in with loads of highly personal questions, you can start by asking people about their likes and dislikes, values, what they feel passionate about, etc.

It's All About *Them*

If you're someone who loves to talk to people and who finds it easy to get others to open up, learning about your Audience will be easy. If you're shy, don't worry. Yes, you'll have to stretch yourself a bit and extend beyond your current comfort zone, but you'll also find that your self-confidence will increase as you become more accustomed to talking to your Audience. Most importantly, you'll lose your self-consciousness if you focus your attention on your Audience. In other words, make it all about *them*, not you.

Why do people spend billions of dollars every year on coaching? Because they get 100% of a coach's time focused on them. In a coaching session, I focus all of my attention on absolutely nothing but my client. Who else in your life does this? As you talk with your Audience, you may have the subtle ulterior motive of getting the information you need to better define your leadership personal brand, but if you remain 100% focused on your Audience during the course of your conversation, it's guaranteed to go smoothly. After all, who doesn't love that kind of attention?

When you talk with your Audience, resist the urge to bring the focus back to yourself. Chances are, you'll be surprised to learn how often you have the impulse to do just that, but every time you shift the focus back to yourself, you lose the opportunity to find out more about your Audience. Bite your tongue even if you hear something you believe to be wrong or something that annoys you. Remain focused on your mission: getting detailed information about your Audience.

Let's say that you have your questions prepared, but you are unable to get a meeting with that all-important person. Once again, make it all about them. If you let your boss or your colleague know that you want his or her advice or input, you have a much better chance of being able to set up that conversation.

Here's an example from the corporate world to demonstrate what I mean. You call prospective customers and ask to get together to discuss your products. If they believe it's just another sales pitch, they will probably see no reason to agree to meeting. If, on the other hand, you tell your prospective customers that you'd like to schedule a meeting to get ideas from them about how your products could be improved to better meet your customers' needs—bingo! Your chances of getting these meetings are much higher because they are now about what will benefit your prospective customers and not about getting their money in your pocket. You've brought the focus of getting together back to your Audience. Again, it's all about them.

A Personal Example from the Front Line

When I was Vice President of International Marketing for Bristol-Myers Squibb's consumer division, we received approval for a very expensive research project to uncover new medical needs in the marketplace. We developed questionnaires and hired a research agency that was all ready to interview dozens of doctors to get the information we needed. One week before the project was to begin, we got bad news: Our budget had been cut by headquarters, so we had no money to carry out the study. It looked like the project was done, kaput, over.

The problem was: We still needed to uncover new medical needs. So, we started brainstorming and reminded ourselves that our sales team was already out in the field every day, trying to sell our brands to the very same doctors who were supposed to have been interviewed by the research agency. The solution became clear but a bit risky: Give the research questionnaires to our sales team, and ask them to give up selling for just one day in order to ask the doctors our research questions instead. This was the first time we had ever tried something like this. So, we took a deep breath, e-mailed the sales team our questionnaires, and waited to see what would happen.

It turned out to be one of the smartest steps we ever took. One after another, salespeople wrote and said, "Thank you! Thank you!" They reported that they had been trying to get certain key doctors to talk openly with them for years, but because the approach they had been using was all about trying to sell products, the doctors remained tight-lipped. This time, when the doctors were asked to talk about what mattered to them—their patients' medical needs—they opened up and shared the exact information we needed. And, in addition, some excellent salesperson-doctor relationships were created as a result.

Never underestimate the power of simply asking questions. It can bridge gaps, foster clearer communication, and create lasting connections.

Hunting for Clues

Let's say you've set up a meeting with your Audience—your boss, a colleague, or your Audience of One who represents a larger group. Now what? You have a list of questions to ask, but you may feel uncomfortable just launching into those questions.

When you enter the room, take a moment. Look around the room for clues that will give you a conversation starter. Are there educational degrees hanging on the wall or family photographs on the desk? Are there vacation photographs or artwork on display? These items give you conversation starters and clues about the individual's personality. A well-placed question like, "I don't know a lot about art, but I really like this piece. What do you know about the artist?" could get your Audience to open up regarding something he or she is passionate about.

Once you've established a rapport, you can begin to ask some of the questions you have planned for your meeting. Of course, don't bombard the person with your questions! Allow time for him or her to give you more details after each question. Practice active listening, and allow the conversation to flow.

Occasionally, your Audience may simply feel stressed about a deadline or a personal matter and may not have time to meet up. If you have trouble getting someone to talk, don't force it. Try again later.

Digging Deep

If asking questions is uncomfortable for you, you could simply share that you're working on defining your leadership personal brand and that you want to ask for input and advice. This is an easy way to begin the question-and-answer process. When you ask your Audience for his or her opinion or advice, it's an automatic compliment. When someone asks *you* for advice, don't you feel respected and honored that your opinion is valued?

What you hear will help you learn a great deal about your Audience. It will also give you the opportunity to ask more questions. Keep an open and objective mind, and really listen. If you've asked for an opinion, take notes as the person speaks. If you're simply having a conversation, concentrate actively on what is said, and take notes now and then.

Ask, Ask Away

Here are some of the questions that you can ask to help you learn more about your Audience's demographics and psychographics. Bear in mind, though, that there is no end to the number of potential questions you could ask. As you listen, be genuinely interested in the answers. That will help you think of new questions in the moment.

Demographic Information
(Provable social characteristics, such as age, sex, income, and education.)

- Where do you live?

- Where did you go to school?

- Are you living where you grew up, or did you move to a new area?

- In what other areas of the country/world (if applicable) have you lived?

- What level of education did you achieve?

- What was the path that got you to your current job?

- How long have you been working at this job?

- What other professions (if any) have you had?

What other demographic-related questions can you think of for your Audience?

Psychographic Information
(More psychologically-oriented personality traits of this person, including attitudes, mindset, etc.)

- What are your priorities in life?

- Where does career fit into those priorities?

- What was behind the choice of your current career?

- What different position in your career do you aspire to (if any)?

- How did your education prepare you for your current career?

- Where have you traveled?

- What are your hobbies and interests?

- How do you spend your spare time?

- What are your favorite foods, music, sports, etc.?

What other psychographic-related questions can you think of for your Audience?

Key Behaviors (Observable manners of behaving or acting)

This is the area that requires observation instead of direct questions. Pay attention to how your Audience behaves, and make note of what their actions say about them. Put on your market-researcher hat, and *watch* your Audience carefully. Be subtle, but pay attention. Take some time to study each person's body language, too, which can give you clues to better understand what your Audience is thinking and feeling.

For example, let's say your Audience is your boss. Does she like to conduct a lot of meetings? If so, what does this say about her personality? Does it mean that she always likes to know what her team is doing? Or does she simply need these meetings in order to feel organized and up to date? How does she conduct meetings? Does she have a set agenda, or does she allow each meeting to take shape in the moment?

Become a Creative Detective

Search the Internet for information about your Audience by typing his or her name into a search engine. What do you find? Articles mentioning the person? Articles by the person? What do these articles tell you about your Audience in terms of demographics, psychographics, and key behaviors?

Social networking sites like LinkedIn, Facebook, and Twitter are also great sources of information. Search for the profiles of your Audience, and read everything you can find. For example, LinkedIn recommendations from others about your Audience can give you clues. Twitter and Facebook can potentially offer you information about this person's hobbies and interests outside of work.

Getting to know your Audience may feel a bit challenging, but look at it this way: People are fascinating. That's why we read novels and watch movies; we all love a good story about people. Think of your Audience's life as a movie, and pretend that you are uncovering it little by little. The more you know about someone, the deeper your relationship, and the more you'll be able to define your leadership personal brand based on the person or people you most want to influence.

Your Leadership Personal Brand Positioning Statement

You're now ready to start completing your Leadership Personal Brand Positioning Statement. To help you with this process, I'll share two examples with you: the Leadership Personal Brand Positioning Statements of two individuals with different jobs and backgrounds. As we work through each chapter, you'll see how these two people have completed each section of their Positioning Statements. These examples can help you understand how your Positioning Statement works, too. Let's start with Kathleen.

Case Study—Kathleen Johnston

Kathleen works as a marketing manager at Consolidated Beverages. When sales of the company's new product line slowed down, her new boss, Josef Kreiss, was hired from outside the company. Now, the company is looking to Josef to rapidly lead his team of marketers in developing many new products and brands.

Kathleen's Leadership Personal Brand Positioning Statement

My Audience consists of:

Demographics (Provable social characteristics of this person, such as age, sex, income, education, etc.): Josef Kreiss, 49, newly-hired Chief Marketing Officer and member of the president's senior staff. Josef has a lot of experience marketing beverages and has an industry-wide reputation for coming up with great new business-building products. In fact, his mission at Consolidated is to speed up the new product development process. He works an average of 12 hours per day.

Psychographics (More psychologically-oriented personality traits of this person, including attitudes, mindset, etc.): Josef is passionate about marketing, especially the creation of new ideas, products, promotions, etc. He needs to get the results he was hired for, but he must also be able to play the politics of the boardroom. In other words, he needs to maintain good relationships with his fellow function heads, while pushing all of them to do new things faster. Josef is confident in his ability to develop high potential ideas and to motivate his team to reach stretching goals. He sees himself as a "player-coach winner."

Key Behaviors (Observable manners of behaving or acting): Josef doesn't really like meetings all that much. In fact, he thinks most meetings take up valuable creative time, so he prefers to keep an open-door and roam-the-halls policy. He often drops in on direct reports from his team (and sometimes even on their subordinates) to see and hear what ideas are popping up and how action plans are coming along. As someone new to the company, Josef needs a senior marketer he can really rely on to be a *change agent* in the organization. With a strong "lieutenant marketer" appearing to be the hard charger, Josef can achieve his goals quicker and more skillfully by actively supporting the lieutenant's recommendations in the boardroom.

Case Study—Eric Chang

Eric is a 26-year-old Associate Branch Manager at Hudson International Bank, where he has worked since he finished his undergraduate degree in finance four years ago. When he was hired at Hudson, he was placed in the management development program, a rotational, fast-track, on-the-job training program that exposes high-potential new employees to all major sub-functions within the bank. Eric currently oversees small business and lower-risk personal loans, and his next logical move would be a promotion to personal banker. This is a great assignment that could prepare Eric for becoming a branch manager and eventually moving into higher management within the bank.

Eric's Leadership Personal Brand Positioning Statement

My Audience consists of:

Demographics (Provable social characteristics of this person, such as age, sex, income, education, etc.): Alicia Gomez, age 40, married with no children, with a Bachelor's degree in finance and marketing. She is the branch manager of Hudson's highest-volume suburban bank location, a job she has held for almost ten years. She began her business career right out of college as a teller with a local bank, but after only a couple of years in that position, she moved to a competitive international bank to join their Branch Manager Development Program. Hudson hired Alicia specifically to place her in charge of their #1 suburban branch. She and her teams have been top performers for Hudson ever since.

Psychographics (More psychologically-oriented personality traits of this person, including attitudes, mindset, etc.): One thing is clear about Alicia: She expects excellence—not just from the people who work for her, but also from herself. You could say she's a "driving perfectionist" who takes pride in jobs done well and customers well-served, but she believes there is still a higher level of performance to be reached by the team. As a result, ...

… Alicia makes a great role model for aspiring Hudson managers. She absolutely believes that "customers are king," making sure each customer feels like so much more than just a number. Alicia expresses this respect every single day in her direction to the team and by her own personal example.

Key Behaviors (Observable manners of behaving or acting): Alicia is definitely a "management by objectives" kind of leader. She and each of her team members sit down and agree in writing about projects and personal development goals. She reviews these projects and assignments regularly with her team to make sure higher performance levels are reached. She also holds a number of training seminars with the team throughout the year. Some of these she leads herself, and others are led by local business leaders. Even though Hudson employees are technically expected to work a set number of hours each week, Alicia works "however many hours it takes" to get things done ahead of schedule and satisfy all customer needs. She doesn't come across as a workaholic, but instead as someone who is genuinely committed to excellence. Given her own work ethic, Alicia will only promote employees to the personal banker level who exhibit a similar passion for excellent work and service, as well as complete dependability. When she *is* able to promote someone with these traits, she takes personal pride in having helped that team member reach a higher goal.

YOUR Leadership Personal Brand Positioning Statement

Get the idea? It's your turn now. Add the name of your Audience, along with the demographics, psychographics, and behaviors that you have discovered about that person. Remember: Your Audience may consist of your boss, a key internal customer, a colleague, or it may be an Audience of One—the individual you feel most represents a larger Audience group.

YOUR Leadership Personal Brand Positioning Statement

My Audience consists of:

Demographics (Provable social characteristics of this person, such as age, sex, income, education, etc.):

Psychographics (More psychologically-oriented personality traits of this person, including attitudes, mindset, etc.):

Key Behaviors (Observable manners of behaving or acting):

It isn't enough just to know thoroughly *who* your Audience is. You also have to know what your Audience *needs*. And that brings us to the next positioning element.

Define it

O u t s i d e

2

Need

Step 1

5

Leadership Personal Brand Positioning Element #2: *Need*

*Before you build a better mousetrap, it helps to know
if there are any mice out there.*

> — Yogi Berra, professional baseball player
> and manager

Brand marketers shouldn't build a better mousetrap unless they know there are people out there with a problem who will *need* that mousetrap. Otherwise, they'll end up with a warehouse full of traps and no one to buy them.

Leadership personal branding is no different. That's why the next step in defining your leadership personal brand is to take all of the information you've gathered about your Audience and figure out what they *need*. This is the heart of it all.

Fix the Problem

Needs are an important part of each and every product brand that exists out there. What do we mean by a Need? Well, there are three ways a smart marketing team would look at Needs for a brand like Nike or Nestle:

- A problem that requires a solution,
- A problem that is currently not being met well enough in the marketplace, and/or
- A new problem that we didn't even know existed.

Here are a few examples of brands that provided a solution to a problem:

- Pert Shampoo (called Wash & Go or Rejoice in some countries) was the first brand to come out with a shampoo and conditioner in one bottle. What Need did it fulfill? The Need for speed and convenience in the morning in order to get out the door faster.
- When Apple discovered that consumers needed a more user-friendly computer, it developed the Mac.
- Viagra was the first drug to solve the problem of erectile dysfunction.

What about a Need that isn't currently being met well enough? This is an example of Yogi Berra's proverbial "better mousetrap."

- Gillette created a razor that gives you a closer shave.
- Colgate Total was the first toothpaste to meet multiple oral care Needs with only one formula.
- While Viagra tackled erectile dysfunction, Levitra did it one better when it proved it could provide erections for a full 24 hours.
- Cialis then fulfilled yet another Need in the marketplace when it announced it could help provide erections for 36 hours, causing the drug to be dubbed "the weekender." How's *that* for a better mousetrap?

Then, there are the Needs we didn't even know we had. Who knew we needed to carry around tiny contraptions that would hold every song we could possibly ever want to hear, plus videos, podcasts, and more? Apple did, and so it created the iPod.

Likewise, many years ago, there was a young man named Howard Schultz, who was the marketing director of a small coffee roasting company. He visited several coffee bars in Italy and noticed that they offered much more to their customers than just coffee. They gave people a place to meet where they could sit for long periods of time and talk. Customers weren't being rushed out the door in order to let someone else have their table. They could relax and spend quality time together. Schultz saw a Need that most of the world didn't even know existed, and Starbucks was born.

When Your Audience's Needs Change

Jonathan was a Swiss CFO in a small but growing European industrial services company. The president owned the company, and Jonathan was second in command. In his five years with the firm, the company grew from 50 to 425 employees as he and his boss negotiated for and purchased other industrial services companies in three neighboring countries. Jonathan loved the fast pace, the constant travel, and the wheeler-dealer nature of the business. It was exactly what he felt he was meant to do with his MBA from INSEAD.

The company did so well, in fact, that the next thing Jonathan and his boss knew, it was *their* company that was being purchased by a large international bank in a multimillion-dollar deal. This brought new experiences to Jonathan that he loved, such as working with savvy investment bankers. Jonathan was also a small shareholder in the company, so he earned a nice lump-sum payout as part of the sale, which was a well-deserved bonus for his frequent 15-hour work days.

Within a matter of weeks after the sale of the company, however, Jonathan noticed that the relationship with his boss started to go sour. His boss began to make snide comments that Jonathan wasn't living up to expectations, and he chided Jonathan about late reports and other tasks. This continued for a while until, one day, Jonathan was called into his boss's office where he was given the news—*"You're fired."*

In order to determine what happened, Jonathan and I sat down and constructed his Leadership Personal Brand Positioning Statement. We soon realized that Jonathan's Audience (in this case, his boss) had developed *new* Needs as a result of the sale of the company. Before the sale, Jonathan's boss had been the full owner and primary shareholder of the company—the one who called the shots and who wanted to expand the business and buy other companies. Now, Jonathan's boss had become just another employee of a large bank, who was responsible for delivering revenues to the new owner. Jonathan's Audience went from needing an entrepreneurial, wheeling-dealing CFO to needing more of an operational CFO—someone who could manage the stable, day-to-day finance and accounting work required by the more traditional new shareholders. Because Jonathan didn't notice this change and was never asked to make adjustments, his efforts no longer responded to his Audience's Needs.

Fortunately, Jonathan was able to seek out another Audience in a new company that could appreciate and benefit from his fast-paced financial savvy, which allowed him to continue working in the style that made him happiest. But the moral of this story is: Stay on the lookout—even if your Audience doesn't change, your Audience's *Needs* might.

Function and Emotion

In the name-brand world, the Needs of a Target Market come in two forms—functional and emotional.

What are some examples of *functional* Needs? Crest toothpaste fulfills the functional Need of fighting cavities. Gatorade fulfills the need of quenching your thirst. Both of these examples are physical. But a functional Need can also be something non-physical yet still tangible, like the Need for a smaller, lighter-weight digital camera.

On the other hand, *emotional* Needs—as you might suspect—have to do with feelings. Because Crest protects your child's teeth from cavities, it also fulfills an emotional Need of making you feel like a good parent. Your Allianz AG homeowner's insurance policy gives you peace of mind because you know you can replace all of your belongings in case of a robbery or fire.

Which type of Need is most important—functional or emotional? The answer is: both! The best brands are designed to hit both types of Needs smack on the head. Indeed, that powerful combination is what builds the most successful brands. Here are some examples:

◆ Bubble Wrap

Functional Need: Protects your fragile items during shipment.

Emotional Need: Gives you 100% assurance that your cousin Mary's wedding gift will arrive in one piece—not ten.

◆ Viagra

Functional Need: Um … you already know this, right?

Emotional Need: Puts the skip back in a man's step because his loving relationship is once again on track.

◆ Starbucks

Functional Need: Gives you a better-tasting cup of coffee.

Emotional Need: Gives you a rewarding coffee experience where you can take a break during the day, have a tasty reward on a comfy couch, check your e-mail on Wi-Fi, and meet your friends for a leisurely chat.

The allure of Starbucks' emotional Need is strong. Think about it: If Starbucks had stopped at only meeting its Audience's functional Need of a better-tasting cup of coffee, it might never have achieved such huge success. After all, there are many great cups of coffee out there.

Just as these name brands make sure they fulfill both the functional *and* emotional Needs of their Target Markets, it's your job as the Brand Manager of YOU™ to make sure you meet both the functional and emotional Needs of *your* Audience. So, how exactly does this tried-and-true branding concept apply to your leadership personal brand?

Functional Needs at Work

First, like any good Brand Manager, you'll want to figure out your Audience's *functional* Needs. In leadership personal branding, functional Needs are typically described as the roles you play—the services you provide in your job. Think of it as a combination of the tasks listed in your job description along with your job title: tax accountant, human resources manager, operations specialist, finance director, etc. In other words, what were you hired to do? If you're an office manager, you may take care of your Audience's Need for efficient office operations, proper functioning and maintenance of all machines, new administrative personnel hires, maintaining a full cabinet of supplies, etc.

Functional Needs are also related to your knowledge, experience, and expertise. If you're hired as a graphic designer, it's automatically expected that you're going to be creative. If your job title is Public Relations Director, it just goes without saying that you will have a full contact list with dozens of great connections.

Emotional Needs at Work

But how do you apply *emotional* Needs to YOU™? Let's revisit famous name brands again. When you're loyal to a particular brand year after year, you've gone beyond just the functional or physical Needs that a brand fulfills for you. You have entered "Brand Land"—the place where a brand has made a true *emotional* connection with you. For example, a while back, a participant in one of my leadership personal branding workshops admitted she was so dedicated to her L'Oreal skin cream that she said, "They'll have to pry it from my cold, stiff fingers once I'm gone!" Now, *that's* a strong emotional brand connection.

Take me as another example: I've been using the same brand of toothpaste every day for more than 20 years. For perspective, I've only been married to my husband for fifteen years ... so, statistically, I've had a longer relationship with my toothpaste than with my husband! When you can make that kind of emotional connection with your Audience, that's when you know you've created true brand loyalty.

Okay, so you aren't a brand of toothpaste, but that's exactly why it will be easier for YOU™ to build an emotional connection with your Audience as you create your desired leadership personal brand. Have you ever had the experience where someone in your company or someone from a nearby department kept coming back to you, asking you to do more work for them? That's most likely because you met that person's emotional Need by building a relationship founded on credibility and trust. The functional Need you met was the work you actually did, but more than that, this person knew that you would deliver quality work on time, again and again. Just like with my favorite toothpaste, *that's* powerful branding.

What Needs Can YOU™ Fulfill?

Functional Needs. First of all, think about what functional Needs you fulfill on the job. These will be made up of the types of work you regularly do. What tasks are listed on your job description? What are your responsibilities at work? Make a list of all of the possible functional Needs you can fulfill.

Emotional Needs. What are your Audience's emotional Needs? Looking at the list below, which of these do you think your Audience most requires from you? What other emotional Needs can you add to the list?

Trust	Honesty	Sincerity
Resourcefulness	Empathy	Encouragement
Creativity	Self-reliance	Diligence
Dynamism	Responsibility	Assertiveness
Reliability	Energy	Sense of Humor
Flexibility	Enterprise	Dedication
Objectivity	Tenacity	Thoroughness
Optimism	Patience	Conscientiousness
Imagination	Versatility	Determination
Tolerance	Intensity	Cooperation
Eagerness	Persuasiveness	Decisiveness
Loyalty	Dependability	Commitment

Once you have a full list, think about which of these Needs your Audience most requires from you, and choose what you believe to be the top two or three.

You may discover unfulfilled Needs through your own observations, but you can also ask your Audience directly about what he/she needs. You might ask, "What do you need from me to make your job easier? What problems do you face that I might be able to solve?" You don't have to ask your Audience to break down their Needs into functional and emotional categories. Once you have their answers, you can separate them into those categories yourself. But your initiative and desire to help will already demonstrate that you are resourceful and cooperative.

Also, don't forget to think about what level of expertise or knowledge is required to fulfill your Audience's functional and emotional Needs. For example, a senior tax accountant will, by the very nature of the job, be required to fulfill different Needs than a new-hire tax accountant straight out of university. Do you have the necessary experience to meet your Audience's Needs, or should you get some more training? Your Audience may have some Needs that you aren't able to fulfill, and that's okay. Your job is to find the Needs that you *can* fulfill and that you *want* to fulfill.

Your leadership personal brand must fit with your experience, knowledge, talents, and expertise. Don't try to squeeze yourself like a square block into a round hole. Once you've figured out your Audience's Needs, you can then define how your leadership personal brand will fulfill one or more of those Needs while staying true to both you and YOU™.

Your Leadership Personal Brand Positioning Statement

So, what does *your* Audience Need? Let's check in with our two colleagues, Kathleen and Eric, to see how they completed this section of their Leadership Personal Brand Positioning Statements. You can use their statements as a guide to help you complete the Needs section of your own statement.

Kathleen's Leadership Personal Brand Positioning Statement

Marketing Manager at Consolidated Beverages

My Audience's Needs are:

Functional:
A highly creative and assertive senior marketer who can take on the role of new product development change agent so that Josef and his innovation team can deliver winning new ideas to Consolidated Beverages.

Emotional:
Someone Josef can trust to absorb the knocks that come with the task, without becoming discouraged.

Eric's Leadership Personal Brand Positioning Statement

Associate Branch Manager at the Hudson International Bank

My Audience's Needs are:

Functional:
A "Mr. Dependable" Personal Banker to serve as a second-in-command at the branch—someone who is dependable and will work however many hours it takes, who sets a standard of excellence in customer service, and is dependable in co-motivating the entire team.

Emotional:
A feeling of pride in seeing younger Hudson up-and-comers perform at higher levels than they sometimes believe they can.

Hopefully, these examples will help you apply what you've learned about your Audience's Needs to your own Leadership Personal Brand Positioning Statement. How well can you fulfill your Audience's Needs, and how can it help you highlight what you have to offer on the job?

YOUR Leadership Personal Brand Positioning Statement

My Audience's Needs are:

Functional:

Emotional:

Define it

O u t s i d e

3

Comparison

Step 1

6

Leadership Personal Brand Positioning Element #3: *Comparison*

Sometimes you can't see yourself clearly until you see yourself through the eyes of others.

— Ellen Degeneres, comedian and TV show host

Now that you have defined the Audience and Needs for your leadership personal brand, you're ready to move on to Comparison—the third of six key elements that define what your brand is all about. At the end of this chapter, you'll be halfway through completing your leadership personal brand definition.

Remember how I defined leadership personal branding? It's the way you want people to perceive, think, and feel about you as a leader *in relation to other leaders*. The Comparison element is where the "in relation to other leaders" part comes into play.

For marketers who manage big name brands, this element is called the "Competitive Framework." That's because name brands compete with each other for a share of the profits in the marketplace. There are only so many buyers of shampoo in the world, so, for example, Pantene and Sunsilk will each command a certain share of the "shampoo pie." The makers of each brand will always look for new ways to make their piece of the pie bigger, shrinking their competitors' shares.

But in leadership personal branding, there is no "market share," so this is where personal brands and name brand products are fundamentally different.

When You Are *Not* Like a Product Brand

In leadership personal branding, if you have a piece of the pie, it doesn't mean you've taken someone else's portion. As human beings, we are simply more multi-dimensional than product brands. Every one of us is unique. You are an individual, and it's up to you to define your own specific leadership personal brand and what role it will play in your career and your self-leadership in the workplace.

To show you what I mean, let's think again about celebrities. Yes, it's possible that Ashton Kutcher and Hugh Jackman could compete for the same part in a film, but each of them would bring something entirely different to that role. You can see why leadership personal branding is not so much about *competition* as it is about *comparison*.

Yet, your leadership personal brand exists in relation to others, so no matter what you do, Comparison *is* an inherent part of how you define it. But who are you compared with? The answer is: all of the people your Audience might consider when they have a Need that must be fulfilled. For example, if you offer tax advice, what other tax accountants could be chosen to do the job instead of you? And don't forget about the importance of emotional Needs. If two tax accountants are equally as good at fulfilling the *functional* Need, your Audience will choose the one who fulfills the *emotional* Need best, such as the accountant who is the most reliable or the individual with the best "can-do" personality.

What can you do to give yourself a "comparative" edge?

Your Leadership Personal Brand Comparison

If I asked you, "What is Heineken?" you'd answer, "It's a beer." In name branding, *what* a brand is or how you normally view the brand is often called the Standard Identity of that brand. For example:

- Nikon is a ... *camera.*

- Listerine is a ... *mouthwash.*

- Harley-Davidson is a ... *motorcycle.*

Similarly, in leadership personal branding, it would be easy to fall into the trap of seeing yourself as only your job title or job description. Are you a:

- Human Resources Executive?

- Sales Representative?

- Media Coordinator?

- Financial Controller?

But those titles don't tell you very much. They're just the tip of the iceberg.

When YOU™ Are More Than You

What could be less distinctive than a leadership personal brand of, say, "Sales Representative"? That label doesn't make you stand out from anyone else. That's why you need to create what I call a "Desired Identity." Your Desired Identity will allow you to go beyond just a standard ol' job title. It's all about getting creative in how you think of yourself and how you could be compared with others who hold the same position.

Great brand managers do this with the brands they manage. If Heineken only positioned itself as "a beer," it wouldn't sell very well. If Nikon was a manufacturer of just any camera, why would anyone choose it over another brand?

Richard Czerniawski and Mike Maloney, marketing colleagues of mine and partners in the U.S.-based firm Brand Development Network International, label this process the "Perceptual Competitive Framework" of a brand. Here are some well-known product brand examples of Perceptual Competitive Framework:

Starbucks isn't just a coffee restaurant … it's a *rewarding coffee experience.*

Gatorade isn't just a thirst quencher … it's the *ultimate liquid athletic equipment.*

Snickers isn't just a candy bar … it's a *between-meal hunger satisfier.*

McDonald's isn't just a fast food restaurant … it's a *fun family food destination.*

Expand Your Thinking

Let's look at this another way and stretch our minds a bit using an exercise called:

When is an apple not a fruit?

If you looked at an apple as just a fruit, then you would naturally compare it to other fruits like grapes, bananas, or oranges.

But what if you looked at an apple as "a portable, ready-to-eat snack?" (And it is, of course!) If you did that, the apple could then be compared to other snack foods like cookies, granola bars, and potato chips.

Now, let's think of an apple as "a daily health maintenance provider" (referring to the old saying that "an apple a day keeps the doctor away"). If you thought of an apple in that way, it could then be compared to vitamin supplements, exercise, and getting plenty of sleep.

But wait! You could also think of an apple as "a beautiful table-top decoration." (If you could see my mother's dining room table, you would know this was true.) Looking at it that way, you could also compare it to candles and flowers. Get the idea?

If you can get your Audience to think about YOU™ in that same expanded way, you can potentially fulfill all sorts of Needs you hadn't even thought of yet. And that's what can help you advance in your career, even if someone else appears to have better credentials and experience. Now *that's* a "comparative" edge.

Who Do YOU™ Want To Be?

Think about how you want to be viewed, and let your imagination go. How can you change the perception of YOU™ from, say, a "store manager" to the Desired Identity of the "Take-Charge Guru"? If you can get your Audience to think about YOU™ that way, and "take-charge attitude" is an important emotional Need of your Audience, you will open yourself up to all sorts of possibilities and opportunities. The "Take-Charge Guru" would become the Desired Identity of your personal brand.

Here are some examples of other potential Desired Identities:

- **The "Get It Done Guy"**—When your division is up against a challenge, people turn to you as the "closer." You are the person they rely on to finish the job.

- **The "Connector"**—You're always networking and know the perfect person for every task. All you need is five minutes to check your contact list.

- **The "Tension Breaker"**—When the tension is high, your coworkers always count on you to tell a joke and bring a smile to everyone's face.

- **The "Innovator"**—When a new idea is needed, everyone comes to you for your imagination and creativity.

- **The "Dynamo"**—When energy and tenacity are called for, you are the first person who comes to mind. You'll keep everyone motivated and on target until the job is done.

- **"Mr. or Ms. Precise"**—When something has to be done right the first time, right down to the last detail, everyone knows your work will be meticulous and exacting.

These are just a few possible Desired Identities. What others can you come up with that would spotlight your specific talents? Brainstorm until you come up with many possibilities, and let your mind run wild without censoring. You never know when a gem might surface.

Think of it this way, and fill in the blanks: I'm not just a store manager; I'm a "Take-Charge Guru."

I'm not just a _____; I'm a _____.

There's More to YOU™ than Meets the Eye

Once you've exercised your imagination, how do you decide which Desired Identity to apply to your leadership personal brand? Go back to the Needs section of your Leadership Personal Brand Positioning Statement. Which one of your potential Desired Identities fulfills your Audience's Needs the best and also sounds the most exciting to you?

When you make your choices, don't think they have to be engraved in stone. As you work through the remaining three elements of your Leadership Personal Brand Positioning Statement, you may discover that you want to adjust your Desired Identity, and that's just fine! For now, however, make a choice that will move you forward in the process of creating your individual brand.

Have Fun With Your Brand!

Nancy is a Senior Administrator, and in her Leadership Personal Brand Positioning Statement, she defined her Desired Identity as, "I'm not just a Senior Administrator; I'm 'The Swiss Army Knife' of the Office Management Team."

While Nancy will probably never actually verbalize this label to anyone, she had fun coming up with this new way of thinking of herself. She likes the idea of being the "Swiss Army Knife" at work. It gives her the opportunity to stand out in her job and make others take notice of who she is, how well she leads herself, and what she has to offer. It's the beginning of a personal brand that can take her far, and it sure beats "Senior Administrator," doesn't it?

The moral of this story? Enjoy the opportunity to be creative as you come up with how YOU™ can be more than just you.

Options, Options, and More Options

Did you know that your Audience's Needs can sometimes be fulfilled by a *what* rather than a *who*? This is how you can extend your "Comparison List."

To complete the Comparison portion of your Leadership Personal Brand Positioning Statement, you will make a list of *all* of the options your Audience has available to satisfy their Needs. Could the Needs be fulfilled by an outside firm? Could a computer program do the work? Could a job or even an entire division be outsourced to another country?

Think about it this way: Let's say you woke up this morning with a backache. What are all the various options available to you to solve that problem? You could:

- Get a massage.

- Go to a chiropractor or osteopath.

- Take a hot bath.

- Use an ice pack or a heat rub.

- Take pain medication.

- Go back to bed.

While a massage therapist would want you to make an appointment for a massage, a pharmaceutical company would want you to buy and take its medication. This is how the pharmaceutical company meets its Audience's Need, and the burden is on the company to convince the Audience that taking medication is the best option to fulfill that Need.

Leadership personal branding works the same way. Your Audience may have many options available that could fulfill their Needs, and it's your responsibility to help them decide that you are the best choice. But first, you need to have an idea of what all your Audience's options are.

Your Audience and its Extended Options

Go back to the Needs section of your Leadership Personal Brand Positioning Statement. What people or options does your Audience have to fill each of those Needs? Think outside the box. This is your Audience's Complete Comparison List that you'll add to your Leadership Personal Brand Positioning Statement. Here are some examples:

Example of an Audience Need:

Develop creative new product ideas

Complete Comparison List:

- Well-known outside "Idea Consultants."

- Senior creative people at various agencies.

- New product "launchers" who have published articles and books.

Your Leadership Personal Brand Positioning Statement

How did our two colleagues apply these exercises to their own Comparison Lists? Take a look. In each case, the Audiences have many options available to meet their Needs. Both Kathleen and Eric had to think about these options and create new Desired Identities to expand how they want to be perceived.

Kathleen's Leadership Personal Brand Positioning Statement

Marketing Manager at Consolidated Beverages

Comparison

I want to be the brand of *(your Desired Identity—the way you would like to be perceived)*:

"New Ideas Champion," championing the ideas of others within the organization, as well as developing new winning product ideas.

being compared with *(your complete Comparison List, including other options you might be compared with)*:

- Other existing Marketing Directors or people in the organization who could perform similar functions.
- Well-known, outside "Idea Consultants."
- Senior creative people at various agencies.
- New product "launchers" who have published articles and books.

Eric's Leadership Personal Brand Positioning Statement

Associate Branch Manager at the Hudson International Bank

Comparison

I want to be the brand of *(your Desired Identity—the way you would like to be perceived)*:

"Gold Standard Service Champion"

being compared with *(your complete Comparison List, including other options you might be compared with)*:

- Other existing Associate Branch Managers.
- Senior account managers at top financial planning and investment firms.

Now, you're ready to take what you've learned, apply it to your own Leadership Personal Brand Positioning Statement, and complete your Comparison section with your Desired Identity and Comparison List.

YOUR Leadership Personal Brand Positioning Statement

Comparison

I want to be the brand of *(your Desired Identity—the way you would like to be perceived)*:

being compared with *(your complete Comparison List, including other options you might be compared with)*:

I hope this chapter sparked your creativity and opened your mind to the many ways you can fulfill your Audience's Needs and win at the Comparison game.

Define it

Strengths

4

I
n
s
i
d
e

Step 1

7

Leadership Personal Brand Positioning Element #4: *Unique Strengths*

Every person born into this world represents something new, something that never existed before, something original and unique.

— Martin Buber, 20th century philosopher and author

If someone who knows you at work was stopped in the middle of the street and asked, "What does _____ [insert your name here] stand for?" What would this person say about you? What would they share that is specific to who you are and what you can do? These are your Unique Strengths. They are the nuts and bolts of your leadership personal brand—where the rubber hits the road when it comes to branding yourself.

In the world of name brands, Unique Strengths are called the "Benefits" that a product offers—the most meaningful promise that a brand can, and wants to, own in the mind of its Target Market. Let's take a recognizable brand as an example. When you hear the name Volvo, what comes to mind? For most people around the world, it's "safety." That is the Benefit that sets Volvo apart from Mercedes Benz, Tata, Toyota, and every other car brand on the market.

How does this apply to leadership personal branding? Just like defining what is unique to Volvo, you have to ask yourself what you bring—or *can* bring—to your job that is different and unique to you.

Consider This

When I speak professionally on the topic of leadership personal branding, an audience member will inevitably approach me and say, "Brenda, the truth is: I'm not really all that unique. I don't think that what I have to offer is distinctive. My contributions aren't any different from anybody else's." And, occasionally, nothing I say seems to be able to change that person's mind.

But then, I bought a Toshiba laptop computer that brought home the point of how unique each one of us truly is. That new computer came with biosensor fingerprint identification. That means the computer had software that recorded and recognized my fingerprint, then used my fingerprint as the "password" for accessing my keyboard, hard drive, bookmarked log-in webpages, etc. No other fingerprint would do! It had to be *my* finger and mine alone.

Besides being a great protective mechanism for my computer, that example also served as a constant reminder that each one of us is unique. Every time I started my computer with my fingerprint, I thought to myself: "No one else on the face of the planet can do that!" I was the only individual out of the 7 billion+ people on earth who could simply "swish" a finger over the top of that biosensor and unlock that computer. My husband tried, my assistants tried, my family members tried but, nope—it was *my* fingerprint, or it just wouldn't work. How powerful is that?

It reminded me that not only do we all have different fingerprints and DNA, but we all have irreplaceable talents and attributes as well. It's an absolute impossibility that anyone else can contribute to an organization in exactly the same way that you can.

Recognizing what you can offer and learning to leverage it is what personal branding is all about. It's a matter of defining clearly what makes you truly distinctive (beyond your finger-prints). Your individual combination of values, passions, and talents is what unlocks the real YOU™—just like my fingerprint unlocks my computer. It's up to you to discover and celebrate that uniqueness. Then, you will know exactly what you can offer your Audience that no one else can.

Unearthing Your Strengths

So, how do you determine what your Unique Strengths are? There are many ways to nail them down. Allow yourself some quality time to think about what you have to offer, and try these ideas to begin uncovering the Unique Strengths that you already have and that you can use at work:

Pay Attention. Listen carefully to what people say when they talk about you. When you're introduced to someone, what words are used to describe you? How do your friends introduce you to someone new? Have you ever given a presentation or received an award? If so, what Unique Strengths were highlighted when you were introduced? If you haven't been formally introduced recently, do you have any programs or materials from past events that would contain a description of you written by someone else?

Performance Reviews. If you're like most people, you focus on your weaknesses when reading your performance reviews. But if you take some time to review your past evaluations, you might see consistent Unique Strengths that you previously overlooked. What do the comments say about your specific talents? Read between the lines to discover what qualities differentiate you.

Take Personality Profiles and Tests. There are several personality tests that can give you insight into your Unique Strengths, like Myers-Briggs (www.myersbriggs.org). You may unearth new things about yourself in the process of taking these psychological tests. If you purchase the book *Now, Discover Your Strengths,* you can access the computerized quiz at www.StrengthsFinder.com, which will uncover your top five Strengths.

There are many personality tests out there, and I've checked out a few for you. Look for my recommended list in the Self-Awareness Assessments Appendix at the back of this book, and try them out.

Ask Your Friends and Colleagues. You cannot uncover your Unique Strengths only by searching within. You need to ask others to get an outside perspective. Just like you asked questions to get to know your Audience and their Needs, ask your friends and colleagues to tell you what Unique Strengths they think you have. Have them tell you what they believe is exceptional, rare, and special about you. Be sure to make this request of people who know you well, of course, and make them aware that you want honest answers.

Asking for feedback can be uncomfortable, but without it, you will have a very narrow view of your Strengths. Nine times out of ten, others will judge you less harshly than you judge yourself, and they will notice positive aspects of YOU™ that you may have overlooked. So, don't be afraid to ask for feedback—it's a key way to discover the perfect Unique Strengths for your personal brand.

Here are some questions you could ask others. Feel free to add to this list.

- When you think of me, what are the first positive traits that come to your mind?

- What special talents do you think I have?

- What attributes do I have that stand out from others?

- What, if anything, is exceptional or rare about me?

- What would you consider to be my very best qualities?

- What would you recommend to others about me or my work?

- If you were trying to convince someone to hire me, what would you say?

Your Audience Needs YOU™

Here's a fundamental fact when it comes to branding, whether it's for product brands or leadership personal brands: Your Unique Strengths must respond to your Audience's Needs.

If you remember, Needs come in two forms—functional and emotional. So, in keeping with that, your Unique Strengths must also come in those same two forms.

Let's look at Volvo again. *Safety* is the functional Need that Volvo fulfills because its cars have been built to keep you from getting hurt in case you are in an accident. But driving a Volvo also gives you peace of mind, so the brand fulfills an important *emotional* Need as well.

In leadership personal branding, a functional Unique Strength could be something like your ability to provide accurate reports that are very detailed. You might call this "precision." An emotional Unique Strength would be your ability to provide those reports on time, every time. You might list this one as "reliability."

Your Functional Unique Strengths

First, go back and consider the functional Needs of your Audience. Which of your Unique Strengths will best address those Needs? Be honest and realistic about how well your Unique Strengths actually meet your Audience's Needs.

It's okay if you don't have a Strength to match every one of your Audience's Needs. This will tell you what Strengths you will want to work on as you build your leadership personal brand. These will become what we'll call your "*Future* Unique Strengths," and we'll call the Strengths you can already provide your "*Existing* Unique Strengths."

Here's a scale to help you rate how well your functional Unique Strengths actually meet your Audience's functional Needs. Go through each of your Audience's Needs, and choose from 1 through 4:

1 = I cannot respond to this Need at all.

2 = I can respond somewhat to this Need.

3 = I can respond very well to this Need.

4 = I am outstanding at responding to this Need.

Here's an example:

Functional Need of Your Audience:	Accurate financial reporting
Your Functional Unique Strength:	Precision
Your Rating from 1-4:	3

How do *your* functional Unique Strengths rate?

Your Emotional Unique Strengths

Now, let's consider your Audience's *emotional* Needs. Rate how well your emotional Unique Strengths meet your Audience's emotional Needs using our scale:

1 = I cannot respond to this Need at all.

2 = I can respond somewhat to this Need.

3 = I can respond very well to this Need.

4 = I am outstanding at responding to this Need.

Here's an example:

Emotional Need of Your Audience:	Turning financial reports in on time
Your Emotional Unique Strength:	Reliability
Your Rating from 1-4:	4

If you find that your current Strengths don't respond to your Audience's Needs as much as you would like, don't worry. Remember that you will have both Existing and Future Unique Strengths, and your Future Unique Strengths will give you something to work on as you further strengthen your leadership personal brand.

How Did You Do?

Now that you've rated your Unique Strengths against your Audience's Needs, you will fall into one of four categories. Which one best describes your situation?

1. I already have the Unique Strengths that respond to my Audience's Needs, and I already exhibit these Unique Strengths at work.

2. I already have the Unique Strengths that respond to my Audience's Needs, but I don't demonstrate these Unique Strengths at work often enough.

3. I don't have the Unique Strengths that fill my Audience's Needs, but I'm willing to develop them because I can and want to respond to my Audience's Needs.

4. I don't have the Unique Strengths that respond to my Audience's Needs, and if I'm honest with myself, I'm not really willing to develop them because they would be too far away from who I truly am.

If you fall into the first category, congratulations! Your Existing Unique Strengths and your Future Unique Strengths are pretty much the same. All you have to do is continue to leverage your Unique Strengths at work and make sure that your Audience recognizes and appreciates them.

If you fall into the second category, your job is to make sure that your Unique Strengths are expressed and recognized at work. Don't worry—the next section of this leadership personal branding system will show you exactly how to do that.

If you fall into the third category, you have discovered that your Existing Unique Strengths are currently not enough to fulfill your Audience's Needs. That's okay. You may have some work to do, but you can make a plan to develop the Future Unique Strengths you need. You have the willingness and the passion to do it, and you will.

If you fall into the fourth category, the Unique Strengths you have now and the Strengths that you need to develop to fulfill your Audience's Needs are very different. While it may feel discouraging to find yourself in this situation, it's an opportunity to do some soul-searching. You may need to consider finding a different job in your organization or perhaps even seeking a new organization or profession that would appreciate your Unique Strengths better. Either way, you now know that you should find a job and/or an Audience that better matches your Unique Strengths, and you will no doubt be happier for it.

Your Leadership Personal Brand Positioning Statement

Take the time to investigate your Unique Strengths using the suggestions above. Which of your Strengths do you believe you are expressing the most at work? These are your Existing Unique Strengths. Take a look at our colleagues' Leadership Personal Brand Positioning Statements to see the Existing Unique Strengths that each of them has pinpointed. You might find that your Existing Unique Strengths are solid but not as exciting as you'd like, or you may discover that you're not yet expressing your greatest Unique Strengths in your career at all. If this is the case, you can fix that situation when you figure out later in the chapter which Future Unique Strengths you need.

Kathleen's Leadership Personal Brand Positioning Statement
Marketing Manager at Consolidated Beverages

Unique Strengths

My Existing Unique Strengths are:

1. Quick, analytical thinking
2. Creativity
3. Personal leadership within the Marketing Department

Eric's Leadership Personal Brand Positioning Statement
Associate Branch Manager at the Hudson International Bank

Unique Strengths

My Existing Unique Strengths are:

1. Aptitude with numbers, especially for accuracy
2. Easy personal style that makes customers feel comfortable
3. Passion for the banking business

YOUR Leadership Personal Brand Positioning Statement

Unique Strengths

My Existing Unique Strengths are:

A Treasure Hunt for Additional Unique Strengths

If you need to develop *new* Unique Strengths—whether to establish your leadership personal brand in your current job or to find a new job where your desired leadership personal brand might be a better fit— you must uncover or develop some more Strengths.

Try the ideas below to uncover additional Strengths that you didn't even know you had or other Strengths that you would like to work on for your leadership personal brand.

List Your Values. Take stock of what's most important to you. If you value being trustworthy above all else, for example, this may be the Unique Strength that you want to apply to your leadership personal brand. Or, if helping others solve problems is most important to you, this may be the Strength you want associated with your name.

Your list of values will help you determine which of your Strengths hold the most meaning for you. As you create your list, however, make sure to avoid borrowing someone else's values. Sometimes, the values of your peers or parents can get mixed up with your own. It's critically important to make sure the foundation of your leadership personal brand is authentically yours.

List Your Passions. People often do best at the activities they love to do the most, so your Unique Strengths are directly related to what excites you. If you are passionate about your Unique Strengths, that passion will move you forward, help you do well, and allow you to enjoy every minute of it. Yet, we often become so involved in the "shoulds" of life that we forget about our passions.

My passion is branding. I love it, I study it, I know it, and I speak professionally about it. Make a list of the activities and things that make *you* feel enthusiastic and joyful, and don't limit the list to items that are related to business or work. You might find something unexpected among the passions in your life—as my client Dani did.

Listening to Your Passions

Dani and I met at a coaching workshop, and I soon learned that she and her husband were avid horse people. They own a ranch where they keep horses, and they love riding. One day, she and her husband mounted their horses in preparation for a long ride, but her husband's horse refused to budge. This had never happened before. Then, the horse did something that was even stranger: It lifted its head back and gently tapped her husband's chest repeatedly. They couldn't figure out what was wrong until, just a few minutes later, her husband suddenly fell off the horse in the midst of a heart attack.

The horse could apparently sense that something was amiss with Dani's husband and, in an effort to protect him, refused to move. Dani and her husband credit their beloved horse with saving his life because if they had gone on that ride, he might have been too far away to get the immediate medical help he needed.

But a few months later, when Dani and I began working together to define her leadership personal brand, she didn't mention horses at all. After all, she had many talents she was trying to sort through—she was a coach, a yoga instructor, and also had 25 years of experience as a human resources expert. How could horses fit into her work life?

As we continued to list Dani's Unique Strengths, I noticed that she didn't sound all that enthusiastic about most of them. Finally, when I asked her to say the one thing she was most passionate about—off the top of her head and without really *thinking* about it—her answer was quick and from the heart: *horses.*

Through our work together, Dani began to realize that working with horses was very similar to working with a corporate team and that many leadership skills could be learned in the process of working with horses. For example, you have to choose your horse carefully, just as you have to carefully choose team members. You have to learn to work effectively with your horse just like you have to learn to work with your team. So, Dani decided to develop a training program for corporate executives that brought them to her ranch to work with horses and learn these important leadership tools. While this meant that Dani would end up eventually leaving her corporate job, she remained involved with that world by creating her own unique business that assisted other corporate executives.

Dani was able to leverage her true passion—which was a hidden Unique Strength—and carve out a niche around equine-assisted leadership development. The moral of the story? Find ways to use your passions in your leadership personal brand, and think creatively. Look for Unique Strengths that you might not have considered before.

Streamlining Your Strengths—Making Choices

You've scored yourself against your Audience's Needs, you've done a full analysis of all of your Unique Strengths, and you have a good long list of both. Now, it's time to make choices. You have to select which of your Unique Strengths will be the critical ones you want to stand for— the core of your leadership personal brand. Be sure to keep in mind that the Unique Strengths you choose should also respond well to your Audience's Needs.

I know that choosing isn't easy, but as author Peter Drucker said, "Wherever you see a successful business, someone once made a courageous decision." The same holds true for leadership personal branding.

Let's look at Volvo once again as an example. It's easy to remember that the brand stands for safety. If the brand tried to stand for safety, *plus* reliability, beauty, innovative style, and unusual extras, you would lose track. Most product brands try to own no more than one or two specific benefits. Pantene owns healthy and shiny hair. Head & Shoulders owns beautiful, dandruff-free hair. It isn't that these are the *only* benefits these brands can offer. They may also have a nice fragrance, moisturize the hair, repair split ends, etc. But good marketers make choices, and that means sticking to just one or two Strengths that the brand truly wants to—and can—own in the minds of its customers.

It's the same with leadership personal branding. As the Brand Manager of YOU™, you must choose two or three Existing or Future Unique Strengths that you can and want to own. Many people balk at this. They say, "Wait a minute, Brenda! I'm much more multidimensional than that. I have many Unique Strengths, and I want to use all of them at work." And, of course, you *should* use them all, and you will. That doesn't mean you won't work on additional Unique Strengths that you want to develop later on. But which are the Unique Strengths you *most* want to be associated with your brand as a leader at work? You need your Audience to be able to remember what you stand for (whether or not they will ever verbalize it). Your Audience can only retain so much, so you have to be focused and consistent in order to be known and remembered for your Unique Strengths.

As you reflect on your Strengths, think once again about how you would like others to perceive, think, and feel about you. What are the main qualities that you want to pop immediately into the minds of your Audience when they think of YOU™? Who would you like to be, and how would you like to be remembered? Which Strengths are the most meaningful and will differentiate you the most? And do these particular Unique Strengths address your Audience's greatest Needs?

Your leadership personal brand is your legacy. It's an opportunity for you to become the person you most want to be at work by capitalizing on the talents and Strengths you already have and those that you want to develop.

Your Leadership Personal Brand Positioning Statement

Take a look at the Future Unique Strengths of Kathleen and Eric. Then, spend some time with your own list of Unique Strengths until you decide on the two or three most important ones.

If you aren't 100% sure which Unique Strengths to choose, that's okay. Don't expect that you'll have a clear, cohesive brand right away. If needed, you can always change any section of your Leadership Personal

Brand Positioning Statement before you finalize it. For now, just do the best you can based on the work you've done so far. When you finish the process of working with this book from start to finish, you'll have a very good idea of what needs to be adjusted in order to have completely mastered the definition of your leadership personal brand.

Kathleen's Leadership Personal Brand Positioning Statement
Marketing Manager at Consolidated Beverages

Unique Strengths

My Future Unique Strengths are:

1. Assertive cross-functional leader who is able to drive teams to actions through ...

2. ... Out-of-the-box creativity that introduces new ideas and breakthrough products.

3. More cleverly anticipating and finding solutions to cross-functional roadblocks.

Eric's Leadership Personal Brand Positioning Statement
Associate Branch Manager at the Hudson International Bank

Unique Strengths

My Future Unique Strengths are:

1. Unwavering reliability toward getting the job done with excellence (instead of "just" getting it done).

2. Leading by example so that others want to follow.

3. Ability to elicit a sense of pride from the Branch Manager.

Once again, it's your turn to complete your own Leadership Personal Brand Positioning Statement. Even if your Unique Strengths are solid and fill your Audience's Needs, try to build on your Existing Strengths, and challenge yourself to make them even more powerful and unique. The more responsive you are to your Audience's functional and emotional Needs, the more you'll be your Audience's brand of choice.

YOUR Leadership Personal Brand Positioning Statement

Unique Strengths

My Future Unique Strengths are:

I hope that thinking about your Existing and Future Unique Strengths has helped you to realize what you have to offer at work, as well as what you can develop further to become an even better asset in the future.

Define it

? Why

5 Inside

Step 1

8

Leadership Personal Brand Positioning Element #5: *Reasons Why*

To be persuasive we must be believable; to be believable we must be credible ...

> — Edward R. Murrow, U.S. broadcaster and journalist

Y ou're almost finished defining your leadership personal brand! We're on leadership personal brand positioning element number five—your Reasons Why. This refers to the reasons why your Audience should trust that you can deliver your specific Unique Strengths. It's all about *credibility*. Your Reasons Why give your Audience reasons to believe that you can do what you claim you can do.

Returning to product brands again, they have Reasons Why that can take on many different forms. On the next page is a list of some popular brands and the Reasons Why you and I believe those brands can deliver what they promise.

Brand	The Reason(s) Why	Type of Reason(s) Why
Dove	1/4 Moisturizing Cream	Ingredient
Neutrogena	#1 Dermatologist Recommended	Endorsement
Patek Philippe	Watches Are Handmade	Process
Heineken	Europe's #1 Imported Beer	Market Experience
Evian	Water from Source Cachat	Source

In leadership personal branding, your Reasons Why mainly come in three forms:

Education. Maybe you have a degree from a reputable university, or you attended a special training course that makes you especially equipped to deliver your Unique Strengths. Or maybe you went to a seminar that gave you some great insights into your industry.

Experience. Your past work experience can be a powerful Reason Why. Perhaps you've spent many years in your field, or you've written an article or book on a topic related to one of your Unique Strengths. Or maybe you've given lectures, conducted a study, or been involved with a project that makes you particularly qualified to deliver your Unique Strengths.

Endorsements. Someone who knows you well may offer a reference or testimonial that gives your Audience a good reason to believe that you can do what you promise. We all know that in the hiring process, references—which are forms of endorsements—are important. When someone with a good reputation speaks highly of you, it's a powerful Reason Why someone would choose to work with *you* compared to someone else.

The Reasons Behind Your Strengths

A Unique Strength without a Reason Why is like an airplane without wings—it just won't hold up. Think about it: If a brand of shampoo simply said it was the best shampoo on the market, would you believe it? No, you'd want some form of proof that this shampoo is better than the rest. You'd feel better knowing that it contains a new patented ingredient that adds luster to your hair. Or that it's been formulated with a specific vitamin known for keeping hair healthy. Likewise, it's very important that each one of your Unique Strengths has a specific Reason Why in order to earn your Audience's trust.

How many reasons can you think of that would prove to your Audience that you can deliver each of your Unique Strengths? Think about them in terms of the three types mentioned earlier—education, experience, and endorsements. In which category or categories do *your* Reasons Why fall?

Here's an example:

Existing Unique Strength:

Creates innovative software programs.

Existing Reasons Why:

- *Experience:* Ten years of experience in the software development field and participation in the development of two award-winning software programs.

- *Education:* A degree in computer technology from New York University and five years of experience working under the mentorship of one of the top innovators in the field.

Review each of the Unique Strengths you chose from the last chapter, and determine what Reasons Why you have for each. Then, look at your list, and consider objectively whether your Reasons Why are truly strong enough or compelling enough to convince your Audience that you can deliver your Unique Strengths.

If you think they are *not* strong enough or if you want to boost your Unique Strengths further, you might need to develop new Reasons Why. Just as we called your Unique Strengths either "Existing" or "Future," we will also divide your Reasons Why into Existing and Future.

- For your Existing Unique Strengths, you probably already have Existing Reasons Why.

- If you have defined a Future Unique Strength, you will almost surely need one or two (or more) Future Reasons Why to make that Strength believable.

Could Your Existing Reasons Why Be Even Better?

If you believe your Existing Reasons Why aren't enough to prove to your Audience that you can deliver what you promise, what Reasons Why could you integrate into your personal brand? Think in terms of education, experience, and endorsements. What could you do to create stronger credibility to support your Strengths?

Brainstorm possible Reasons Why that would lend support for your Existing and Future Unique Strengths. Allow your mind to be free of judgment at first, and you might discover something surprising. Which ideas make the most sense? Don't choose something that you would hate to do. For example, if sitting through an industry conference sounds like the last thing you'd ever want to do, then find a different Reason Why to support your Unique Strengths.

On the other hand, don't let fear get in your way. For example, if writing an article or a book excites you but also makes you feel challenged and a bit nervous, get the help you need, and just do it!

How many Reasons Why should you choose? The answer depends on the number your Audience will find meaningful. How many Reasons Why do you need to truly differentiate YOU™? Even more importantly, how many can your Audience honestly remember? It's better to keep your Reasons Why to a minimum. Focus on quality, not quantity. The Reasons Why won't matter much if your Audience can't remember them at the precise moment they're considering choosing YOU™ over someone else for an opportunity that has arisen.

It's Research Time

It's important to do some investigation to find out exactly what your Audience requires in order to believe that you can deliver the Unique Strengths you promise. Let's say you're a tax accountant, and you have five years of experience in your field, as well as an undergraduate degree in accounting with a minor in business. The Unique Strength you want to prove to your Audience is "the most knowledgeable of all in-house tax accountants." How can you find out what's required to convince your Audience of this Unique Strength?

- Ask your Audience to tell you exactly what Reasons Why would do the trick. Would it be better to have more experience, more education, or more endorsements?

- Look at other successful accountants in your company. What are *their* Reasons Why?

- Research in-house accountants at other successful firms, maybe even asking one or two of those accountants to lunch in order to find out his or her Reasons Why.

You may discover through your research, for example, that your desired Reasons Why involve obtaining a diploma as a Certified Management Accountant. If this is the case, you have a Future Reason Why to apply to your Leadership Personal Brand Marketing Plan in the next section of the book.

Here's an example of a Unique Strength you might plan to work on and the Reasons Why you can create in the process:

Future Unique Strength:

Creates recognized, best-in-class software programs.

Possible Future Reasons Why:

- *Education:*

  - Regular continuing education to learn new innovations in software development.

  - Attend at least one industry conference around the world every year.

- *Experience:*

  - Initiate a new software development project at work that solves a long-term problem.

  - Write an article for the company newsletter and/or a trade magazine about software development.

Creating a Reason Why

Paul was an attorney in a large law firm in Warsaw, Poland. He found it difficult to get noticed, not only as compared with other attorneys in his same firm, but also as compared with other lawyers in the city. There were so many firms, but specializing didn't really make sense there. In fact, the only way to make a good living in the legal field in Poland was to be a generalist. So, where did this leave Paul?

He decided one way to set himself apart would be to write a book about the legal aspects of doing business in Poland. So, he did the research needed and completed the writing. The book was targeted toward companies from abroad who wanted to expand into the Polish market, and the book created a powerful Reason Why for his audience to believe that Paul would be a good attorney to help set up businesses in the country. Suddenly, he was seen and called upon as an expert because he had demonstrated himself to *be* an expert by writing a book on the topic. As a result of the book, Paul found himself frequently interviewed for magazine articles and asked to speak at conferences, which further strengthened his expert leadership personal brand. What's more, he gained several high-paying clients because more people had heard about him.

The moral of this story is: If you don't already have the Reasons Why you need, *create your own*. Find a way to establish yourself as an expert in whatever you do. This doesn't mean you have to write a book. What else could set you apart in your world? Maybe you could write some articles, take a course, or gain certification to prove that you can truly deliver your Unique Strengths.

Your Leadership Personal Brand Positioning Statement

Let's check in with our colleagues to see how they have applied Reasons Why in their Leadership Personal Brand Positioning Statements.

Kathleen's Leadership Personal Brand Positioning Statement

Marketing Manager at Consolidated Beverages

Reasons Why

My Existing Reasons Why *(why my Audience should believe I can deliver my Unique Strengths)* **are:**

1. Several line extension successes already in the market.
2. Promoted three times in four years at Consolidated.
3. Developed three new business-building consumer promotions.

My Future Reasons Why That I Want to Work on are:

1. Agreement (by Josef) to my breakthrough New Products Rollout Plan in the Strategic Plan presentation.
2. Positive feedback from non-marketing division heads to Josef about my cross-functional leadership abilities.
3. Consistent demonstration of my "can-do" positive attitude.

Eric's Leadership Personal Brand Positioning Statement

Associate Branch Manager at the Hudson International Bank

Reasons Why

My Existing Reasons Why *(why my Audience should believe I can deliver my Unique Strengths)* **are:**

1. Four years of experience in all sub-functions of the bank.
2. Promoted to Associate Branch Manager on schedule.
3. Numerous unsolicited compliments from bank customers (received by the Branch Manager).

Eric's Leadership Personal Brand Positioning Statement

Associate Branch Manager at the Hudson International Bank

Reasons Why (cont'd)

My Future Reasons Why That I Want to Work on are:

1. Volunteering to take on additional Personal Banker types of projects and delivering them ahead of schedule with superior customer service.

2. Taking a more active role in Branch Manager training programs as a team leader when working on training exercises.

3. Ultimately, being promoted to Personal Banker ahead of normal timing.

Perhaps Kathleen's and Eric's choices have given you some ideas about your own Existing and Future Reasons Why?

YOUR Leadership Personal Brand Positioning Statement

Reasons Why

My Existing Reasons Why *(why my Audience should believe I can deliver my Unique Strengths)* **are:**

My Future Reasons Why That I Want to Work on are:

Define it

I
n
s
i
d
e

6

Character

Step 1

9

Leadership Personal Brand Positioning Element #6: *Brand Character*

Attitude is a little thing that makes a big difference.
— Winston Churchill, former British Prime Minister

The final positioning element in Step 1 of the *Master the Brand Called YOU™* leadership personal branding system is Brand Character. Although it may be the last part of your definition, it definitely isn't the least. Your leadership personal Brand Character is incredibly important and can truly differentiate YOU™.

What do I mean by Brand Character? When it comes to name brands, you may not have heard of "Brand Character" before, but it definitely exists. And many of the most successful brands out there use Brand Character to differentiate themselves—Pepsi and Coke, for example. Let's be honest: Both Pepsi and Coke are made up of essentially the same ingredients—carbonated water, sweetener, and flavoring. Yet, absolutely everyone seems to have a do-or-die affinity for one cola over the other. Heck, I've seen people get into big arguments over which one is "the best."

With products like Pepsi and Coke, which have ingredients that are so similar, you can thank their distinctive Brand Characters for the strong brand loyalty consumers have for them. And the players behind those Brand Characters? The smart Brand Managers who develop and manage those brands. Let's face it: The functional Needs that Pepsi and

Coke fill are pretty much the same. They quench your thirst and satisfy your taste buds. But the Brand Character of each creates an *emotional* connection that has taken both brands to unbelievable heights. A brand's Character may be less tangible than the Needs it fulfills, but smart Brand Managers take this element very seriously. It can literally make or break a brand's success.

What are some other brands that are mainly differentiated by Character? Think perfumes, alcohol, and beer just to name a few. Take some time to notice the advertising campaigns for these types of brands, and I think you'll see what I mean. For example, take a look at an ad for Grey Goose Vodka compared with Cuervo Tequila. The Character of Grey Goose is modern, mature, and sophisticated, while Cuervo's Character is youthful, wild, and "party animal." It's actually a lot of fun to discover the Brand Characters communicated in ads and commercials. Start paying close attention, and you will see that Brand Character is a critical element that clearly separates one brand from another.

From Pepsi and Vodka to YOU™

How does Brand Character apply to you and your leadership personal brand? Your Brand Character is the one element in our six Leadership Personal Brand Positioning Statement elements that has as much to do with who you are as what you do. Think of your individual Brand Character as the "personality" of your brand. While your Unique Strengths are *what* you offer to your Audience, your leadership personal Brand Character is more about the *way* you offer those Unique Strengths—your attitude and your prevailing temperament.

How do you talk about personal Brand Character? It's most often described with adjectives in the same way you would describe a person.

Watch Out!

Don't get Brand Character confused with a Unique Strength. A Unique Strength is a noun—it's *what* you can offer. To use a brand name example, Energizer battery's Strength might be "longer-lasting," but the Character of the battery brand would be "reliable" or "never gives up."

Are You a Character?

The first task we need to tackle is to determine your leadership personal Brand Character as it stands right now. In other words, what is the Brand Character you have already presented to others at work either as a self-leader or as a leader of others? One of the best ways to determine these traits is to ask others in your professional life to describe your Brand Character.

Here are some questions you can ask co-workers and colleagues that will give you a better idea of your leadership personal Brand Character. Again, make sure you ask people you trust. These can be tricky questions!

1. What do you consider to be the most positive aspects of my personality?

2. What would you consider to be less positive aspects of my personality?

3. If you were trying to "sell me" to someone, what would say about me?

4. If you were writing my obituary, what would you include?

Describing Your Character

What adjectives describe your leadership personal Brand Character? Include those you heard from the people you asked, and add adjectives you think best describe your unique Character. At first, think about your overall personality rather than just the Character traits you express only at work. The key is to be as specific as possible, and try to think of qualities that aren't the same as everyone else's. Look up words on dictionary.com or thesaurus.com if you need help coming up with more adjectives.

Irreverent	Serene	Dedicated
Rascal	Earnest	Even-tempered
Street-wise	Sparkling	Decisive
Authentic	Soulful	Vivacious
Maverick	Eloquent	Generous
Professional	Soft-spoken	Chic

Focused	Gregarious	Spiritual
Gracious	Grounded	Considerate
Altruistic	Industrious	Sociable
Fair-minded	Courageous	Visionary
Colorful	Approachable	Daring
Magnetic	Whimsical	Ethical
Inspirational	Direct	Compassionate
Engaging	Wise	Encouraging
Influential	Persuasive	Passionate

As you think about this list, consider which of these Character traits are most important—the most true to the authentic YOU™. How many of your Character traits have you expressed openly and comfortably in your career up to this point? Do you communicate these traits at work?

Another Option: Short Narrative

Besides listing words or adjectives to describe your leadership personal Brand Character, you can also develop a short *narrative* that describes it. Using a product brand example, the Brand Character of the powerhouse North American Tide laundry detergent brand could be something like: "The perfectionist who doesn't stop until the job gets done." Switching back to leadership personal branding, an example might be: "The invaluable can-do person you can always count on to take care of what needs to be done." What might be a short narrative descriptor for YOU™?

Let's Get Creative!

You may have hidden some of your personality's strongest characteristics at work, even though they could help you advance if they were communicated as part of your leadership personal brand. Thinking along those lines, let's dig deeper to uncover even more aspects of your Character that you might want to add to your brand.

Keep in mind that aspects of your Character can also be developed, but most of the time, your Brand Character is a fundamental part of who you are. For example, Sandra was working as an Administrative Assistant in a mid-sized law firm. She was doing well in her job, but what she really wanted was to be an Administrative Supervisor at the firm. She learned that the firm looked to their supervisors to continuously develop new ideas for improving office efficiency, and they were then expected to present those ideas in meetings with managing attorneys. All of this meant Sandra would have to be more assertive on the job than she was used to being. Even though she knew it would be hard for her to assert herself that way, it was something she had always wanted to be able to do. She knew she would have to push herself out of her comfort zone if she wanted to get the promotion. For Sandra, it wasn't going to be easy, but she was determined to develop her self-leadership in this respect.

Sandra decided to work on the Brand Character quality of "assertiveness." She became active as a volunteer in her community's visitors bureau and consciously focused on coming up with ideas that would help the bureau run more smoothly. When it came time to share her ideas with others, Sandra had to take a deep breath and muster up the courage. But in the end, several of her ideas were well-received and implemented by the visitors bureau, and with great results. This kind of experience gave Sandra the confidence she needed to let it be known to her superiors that she was interested in becoming an Administrative Supervisor. Even though she hadn't yet had the opportunity to implement any of her efficiency ideas in her law firm work, the community experiences she had gave her several great examples that she could share about improving the visitors bureau's efficiency. She shared those examples with her superiors, and this edge was enough for Sandra to get the promotion she wanted. "Assertive idea generator and implementer" has simply become a part of Sandra's Character. It's now a valued part of the leadership personal brand that she brings to the law firm.

Creative Comparisons

Sometimes, thinking about the attributes of others can give you ideas of qualities you might want to focus on or develop in yourself. Here are three ways to open your imagination to other possible descriptive words that you can use for your personal Brand Character.

1. **Compare yourself to a celebrity.** For example:

   Lady Gaga is … *daring and original* … and so am I.

   Roger Federer is … *focused and dedicated* … and so am I.

Oprah Winfrey is ... *charitable and influential* ... and so am I.

Who could you compare yourself to? Try to think of more than one:

_____ is _____ and so am I.

2. **Compare yourself to a popular name brand.** For example:

The clothing brand I'm most like is Burberry because ... *I'm traditional and reliable.*

The car brand I'm most like is Lamborghini because ... *I'm cutting-edge and state-of-the-art.*

The bookseller brand I'm most like is Amazon.com because ... *I'm fast and have everything at my fingertips.*

What name brands are you most like?

The _____ brand I am most like is _____ because I'm _____.

3. **Compare yourself to a role model.** Think of someone you admire from your local community, such as your Scout leader when you were a child, a favorite teacher, a university advisor, or the mayor of your city.

   • How would you describe this person? As a leader? An honorable person?

   • What characteristics of this individual would you like to develop in yourself?

Narrowing It Down

As you work on finalizing your Brand Character, go back and take a look at the Audience you defined in your Leadership Personal Brand Positioning Statement. Does your current Character seem to "fit" with the wants, needs, and attitudes of your Audience? Will it connect with them? If not, which of your many Character traits can you emphasize at work in order to appeal even more to your Audience?

Note that I used the word "appeal." Remember: Leadership Personal Brand Character is the personality, attitude, and prevailing temperament that you communicate to others. Would your Audience be *attracted to* your Brand Character?

Making the Leadership Personal Brand/ Corporate Brand Connection™

Does your leadership personal brand "connect" with your company's brand? I once coached a bank executive named Divya who had been very happy at her bank for 15 years. She had had great experiences, traveling and living in many different places around the world. Then, a global financial crisis happened, and in the years that followed, Divya slowly found herself becoming more and more uncomfortable at her banking institution and in her job. She was struggling to maintain the level of excitement and contentment at work that she had experienced before.

We worked on defining Divya's personal brand. Once that was finished, we created a Brand Positioning Statement for the bank, then compared Divya's individual brand to the brand of the organization. What did this uncover? While Divya's individual Brand Character had not changed over the years, the *corporate* Brand Character of the bank where she worked had changed a great deal as a result of the financial crisis. It was no longer the friendly, enjoyable place she had loved so much. New rules and much stricter regulations made it a more rigid environment with all sorts of compliance requirements. That altered the whole nature of the workplace as well as the work that Divya was doing.

She came to realize that her individual Brand Character was no longer in sync with the bank's corporate Brand Character. Since she didn't feel she could change the company's Character, she had to ask herself if she felt she could change her *own* Character to fit with the Character of the bank. For her, the answer was "no." Even though she would have liked to stay in her job, it simply wouldn't be healthy or authentic for her to do that given the fundamental disconnect between her own leadership personal Brand Character and the new Brand Character of the bank.

Divya decided to leave the bank and look for employment elsewhere. This may sound like a fairly dramatic step, but the clarity she received by comparing her own Leadership Personal Brand Positioning Statement with the Brand Positioning Statement of her company allowed her to accept a much-needed change.

Reality Check

What happens if *you* discover a disconnect between your own Brand Character and the Character of the place where you work, similar to what happened with Divya?

For example, if you would describe your fundamental leadership personal Brand Character as "outgoing, entrepreneurial, innovative, and energetic," but your Audience is looking for the characteristics of "stable, sticking to status quo, and following established processes," what would you have to do to make an emotional connection with your Audience? And do you really want to make those changes in your leadership personal Brand Character in order to make that connection, or is it time to think about leaving, as Divya did? If you find this to be true in your case, you may have some soul-searching to do in terms of where you are and how that fits with *who* you are.

Keep It Focused and Uncommon

Remember the professional speaker named Gavin from South Africa? He found that his Unique Strengths and Character didn't always appeal to certain Audiences, so he became very specific about the Audiences he wanted to focus on—a decision that saved him time, money, and a lot of potential frustration.

Gavin was also careful to choose a Brand Character for himself that was distinctive and that fully captured what was original about him. He has become known for shaking things up and saying things that may at first throw people off balance. But the end result is that he's a very exciting speaker who helps others think outside the box through what he calls his "irreverent and naughty" Brand Character. Take a lesson from Gavin—is *your* Brand Character far from run of the mill?

Your Leadership Personal Brand Positioning Statement

As you get ready to complete the Brand Character portion of your Leadership Personal Brand Positioning Statement, our colleagues Kathleen and Eric have completed theirs as well. After you've read their Character statements, choose five to six of the most important qualities (attitudes, character descriptors) that you have uncovered to describe YOU™, and add them to your Positioning Statement. These will be the qualities you consider to be your best that will also greatly appeal to your Audience.

If your leadership personal Brand Character is already appealing to your Audience, you're in great shape! If not, you may simply need to make sure that more of your personality traits become known at work. These are the traits that will best appeal to your Audience but that you may be suppressing right now. In bringing these qualities out at work, you will become more true to who you really are.

Kathleen's Leadership Personal Brand Positioning Statement
Marketing Manager at Consolidated Beverages

Brand Character

My Leadership Personal Brand Character *(how I want my leadership personal Brand Character to be perceived, including my overriding attitude, temperament, and personality)* **is:**

A trusted and out-of-the-box creative team leader who never lets up and never lets the team settle for just "good," but spurs on the entire organization to reach higher: a "champion's champion."

Eric's Leadership Personal Brand Positioning Statement
Associate Branch Manager at the Hudson International Bank

Brand Character

My Leadership Personal Brand Character *(how I want my leadership personal Brand Character to be perceived, including my overriding attitude, temperament, and personality)* **is:**

A "gold standard" setter and achiever, completely reliable and committed to excellence in serving.

What Character do you want to bring to your own brand?

YOUR Leadership Personal Brand Positioning Statement

Brand Character

My Leadership Personal Brand Character *(how I want my leadership personal Brand Character to be perceived, including my overriding attitude, temperament, and personality)* **is:**

You've now completed Step 1 by defining all six elements of your leadership personal brand. It's time to combine the elements to fully flesh out your complete Leadership Personal Brand Positioning Statement.

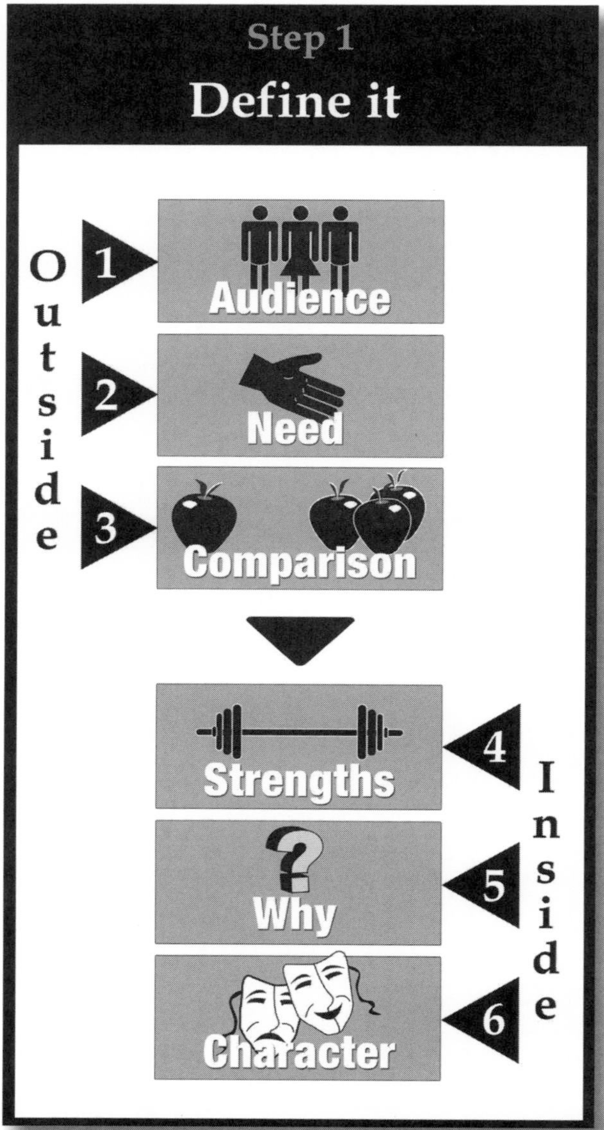
Step 1
Define it
Outside
1 Audience
2 Need
3 Comparison
Inside
4 Strengths
5 Why
6 Character

10

Pulling It All Together: Your Complete Leadership Personal Brand Positioning Statement

Details create the big picture.
— Sanford I. Weill, banker, financier
and philanthropist

Congratulations! You have now defined all six elements of your Leadership Personal Brand Positioning Statement. It's time to pull it all together into a clear and consistent "big picture."

Before we do, though, let's take a look at the fully completed Leadership Personal Brand Positioning Statements of Kathleen and Eric and read them this time with an overall sense of each of their leadership personal brands.

Kathleen's Leadership Personal Brand Positioning Statement

Marketing Manager at Consolidated Beverages

My Audience consists of:

Demographics (Provable social characteristics of this person, such as age, sex, income, education, etc.): Josef Kreiss, 49, newly-hired Chief Marketing Officer and member of the president's senior staff. Josef has a lot of experience marketing beverages and has an industry-wide reputation for coming up with great new business-building products. In fact, his mission at Consolidated is to speed up the new product development process. He works an average of 12 hours per day.

Psychographics (More psychologically-oriented personality traits of this person, including attitudes, mindset, etc.): Josef is passionate about marketing, especially the creation of new ideas, products, promotions, etc. He needs to get the results he was hired for, but he must also be able to play the politics of the boardroom. In other words, he needs to maintain good relationships with his fellow function heads, while pushing all of them to do new things faster. Josef is confident in his ability to develop high potential ideas and to motivate his team to reach stretching goals. He sees himself as a "player-coach winner."

Key Behaviors (Observable manners of behaving or acting): Josef doesn't really like meetings all that much. In fact, he thinks most meetings take up valuable creative time, so he prefers to keep an open-door and roam-the-halls policy. He often drops in on direct reports from his team (and sometimes even on their subordinates) to see and hear what ideas are popping up and how action plans are coming along. As someone new to the company, Josef needs a senior marketer he can really rely on to be a *change agent* in the organization. With a strong "lieutenant marketer" appearing to be the hard charger, Josef can achieve his goals quicker and more skillfully by actively supporting the lieutenant's recommendations in the boardroom.

My Audience's Needs are:

Functional:
A highly creative and assertive senior marketer who can take on the role of new product development change agent so that Josef and his innovation team can deliver winning new ideas to Consolidated Beverages.

Emotional:
Someone Josef can trust to absorb the knocks that come with the task, without becoming discouraged.

Comparison

I want to be the brand of *(your Desired Identity—the way you would like to be perceived)*:

> "New Ideas Champion," championing the ideas of others within the organization, as well as developing new winning product ideas.

being compared with *(your complete Comparison List, including other options you might be compared with)*:

- Other existing Marketing Directors or people in the organization who could perform similar functions.

- Well-known, outside "Idea Consultants."

- Senior creative people at various agencies.

- New product "launchers" who have published articles and books.

Unique Strengths

My Existing Unique Strengths are:

1. Quick, analytical thinking

2. Creativity

3. Personal leadership within the Marketing Department

My Future Unique Strengths are:

1. Assertive cross-functional leader who is able to drive teams to actions through …

2. … Out-of-the-box creativity that introduces new ideas and breakthrough products.

3. More cleverly anticipating and finding solutions to cross-functional roadblocks.

Reasons Why

My Existing Reasons Why *(why my Audience should believe I can deliver my Unique Strengths)* **are:**

1. Several line extension successes already in the market.

2. Promoted three times in four years at Consolidated.

3. Developed three new business-building consumer promotions.

My Future Reasons Why That I Want to Work on are:

1. Agreement (by Josef) to my breakthrough New Products Rollout Plan in the Strategic Plan presentation.

2. Positive feedback from non-marketing division heads to Josef about my cross-functional leadership abilities.

3. Consistent demonstration of my "can-do" positive attitude.

Brand Character

My Leadership Personal Brand Character (*how I want my leadership personal Brand Character to be perceived, including my overriding attitude, temperament, and personality*) **is:**

A trusted and out-of-the-box creative team leader who never lets up and never lets the team settle for just "good," but spurs on the entire organization to reach higher: a "champion's champion."

Eric's Leadership Personal Brand Positioning Statement

Associate Branch Manager at the Hudson International Bank

My Audience consists of:

Demographics (*Provable social characteristics of this person, such as age, sex, income, education, etc.*): Alicia Gomez, age 40, married with no children, with a Bachelor's degree in finance and marketing. She is the branch manager of Hudson's highest-volume suburban bank location, a job she has held for almost ten years. She began her business career right out of college as a teller with a local bank, but after only a couple of years in that position, she moved to a competitive international bank to join their Branch Manager Development Program. Hudson hired Alicia specifically to place her in charge of their #1 suburban branch. She and her teams have been top performers for Hudson ever since.

Psychographics (*More psychologically-oriented personality traits of this person, including attitudes, mindset, etc.*): One thing is clear about Alicia: She expects excellence—not just from the people who work for her, but also from herself. You could say she's a "driving perfectionist" who takes pride in jobs done well ...

My Audience consists of: (cont'd)

… and customers well-served, but she believes there is still a higher level of performance to be reached by the team. As a result, Alicia makes a great role model for aspiring Hudson managers. She absolutely believes that "customers are king," making sure each customer feels like so much more than just a number. Alicia expresses this respect every single day in her direction to the team and by her own personal example.

Key Behaviors (Observable manners of behaving or acting): Alicia is definitely a "management by objectives" kind of leader. She and each of her team members sit down and agree in writing about projects and personal development goals. She reviews these projects and assignments regularly with her team to make sure higher performance levels are reached. She also holds a number of training seminars with the team throughout the year. Some of these she leads herself, and others are led by local business leaders. Even though Hudson employees are technically expected to work a set number of hours each week, Alicia works "however many hours it takes" to get things done ahead of schedule and satisfy all customer needs. She doesn't come across as a workaholic, but instead as someone who is genuinely committed to excellence. Given her own work ethic, Alicia will only promote employees to the personal banker level who exhibit a similar passion for excellent work and service, as well as complete dependability. When she *is* able to promote someone with these traits, she takes personal pride in having helped that team member reach a higher goal.

My Audience's Needs are:

Functional:
A "Mr. Dependable" Personal Banker to serve as a second-in-command at the branch—someone who is dependable and will work however many hours it takes, who sets a standard of excellence in customer service, and is dependable in co-motivating the entire team.

My Audience's Needs are: (cont'd)

Emotional:
A feeling of pride in seeing younger Hudson up-and-comers perform at higher levels than they sometimes believe they can.

Comparison

I want to be the brand of *(your Desired Identity—the way you would like to be perceived)*:

"Gold Standard Service Champion"

being compared with *(your complete Comparison List, including other options you might be compared with)*:

- Other existing Associate Branch Managers.

- Senior account managers at top financial planning and investment firms.

Unique Strengths

My Existing Unique Strengths are:

1. Aptitude with numbers, especially for accuracy.

2. Easy personal style that makes customers feel comfortable.

3. Passion for the banking business.

My Future Unique Strengths are:

1. Unwavering reliability toward getting the job done with excellence (instead of "just" getting it done).

2. Leading by example so that others want to follow.

3. Ability to elicit a sense of pride from the Branch Manager.

Reasons Why

My Existing Reasons Why *(why my Audience should believe I can deliver my Unique Strengths)* **are:**

1. Four years of experience in all sub-functions of the bank.

2. Promoted to Associate Branch Manager on schedule.

3. Numerous unsolicited compliments from bank customers (received by the Branch Manager).

My Future Reasons Why That I Want to Work on are:

1. Volunteering to take on additional Personal Banker types of projects and delivering them ahead of schedule with superior customer service.

2. Taking a more active role in Branch Manager training programs as a team leader when working on training exercises.

3. Ultimately, being promoted to Personal Banker ahead of normal timing.

Brand Character

My Leadership Personal Brand Character *(how I want my leadership personal Brand Character to be perceived, including my overriding attitude, temperament, and personality)* **is:**

A "gold standard" setter and achiever, completely reliable and committed to excellence in serving.

YOUR Leadership Personal Brand Positioning Statement

My Audience consists of:

Demographics:

Psychographics:

Key Behaviors:

My Audience's Needs are:

Functional:

Emotional:

Comparison

I want to be the brand of *(your Desired Identity—the way you would like to be perceived):*

being compared with *(your complete Comparison List, including other options you might be compared with):*

Unique Strengths

My Existing Unique Strengths are:

My Future Unique Strengths are:

Reasons Why

My Existing Reasons Why *(why my Audience should believe I can deliver my Unique Strengths)* **are:**

My Future Reasons Why That I Want to Work on are:

Brand Character

My Leadership Personal Brand Character *(how I want my leadership personal Brand Character to be perceived, including my overriding attitude, temperament, and personality)* **is:**

Is Your Statement Complete?

As you sit back and look at the work you've done, be sure to double-check that your Positioning Statement has all of the information it needs:

1. **Audience**
   - Does your statement have all of the elements of a well-defined Audience? When you read it, do you really feel that you "know" your Audience?

2. **Needs**
   - Are the Needs listed the ones you honestly believe to be the most important for your Audience?
   - Did you list both functional *and* emotional Needs of your Audience?

3. **Comparison**
   - Does your Comparison List go beyond the obvious and include many other options?
   - Do you have a clearly defined, unique Desired Identity?

4. **Unique Strengths**
   - Do you have two to three clearly defined Unique Strengths that you know you want to—and can—own? Are they truly the most important Strengths for YOU™?
   - Do your Unique Strengths respond to both the functional and emotional Needs of your Audience?

5. **Reasons Why**
   - Are your Reasons Why strong enough to be convincing to your Audience? Will they truly prove that you can deliver the desired Unique Strengths that you've stated for yourself?
   - Do you need to develop Future Reasons Why to better support your Future Unique Strengths?

6. **Leadership Personal Brand Character**
   - Is your leadership personal Brand Character in sync with your Audience's psychographics, attitudes, and beliefs?
   - Based on what you know about your Audience, would your Brand Character be appealing?

Get Feedback

Before you sign off on your Positioning Statement, I encourage you to get some objective opinions.

1. Show your Leadership Personal Brand Positioning Statement to others you trust, and ask for their comments. Do they agree that it presents a great brand for you, knowing what they know about you? When you achieve that desired leadership personal brand, do they believe your vision for the brand will be strong enough to help you gain what you want to achieve, such as a promotion, higher salary, or the recognition you want?

2. If you really think it would help, show your Leadership Personal Brand Positioning Statement to your Audience. What's your Audience's reaction? Remember: Only do this, of course, if you believe it won't undermine your relationship! Most of the time, you wouldn't share your Positioning Statement that openly. Remember: You've never seen Starbucks' Positioning Statement, correct? But if you *do* have the right kind of relationship with your Audience, go for it.

3. Visit www.brendabence.com/books-products/ and, for a small fee, you can download a helpful "e-audit" form that will walk you through a number of additional questions to think about as you finalize and review your Leadership Personal Brand Positioning Statement.

"OK, now it's time to share feedback......"

How Does It Look?

Now that you can sit back and see the big picture, how do you feel about your leadership personal brand? Does it feel "right" to you? Is your statement on target, and does it accurately tell your story? On a scale from 1 to 10, how well does your statement really communicate who YOU™ are and who YOU™ want to be as a self-leader and/or a leader of others? If you don't think you can score your statement at around at least an 8 or 9, take some more time to reflect on the various elements and consider how you might improve them. It's fundamental to get this part right, so be sure to devote the time you need to feel as good about your leadership personal brand definition as possible.

Maybe you can't score your statement as high as you would like because you still have some work to do to truly embody the brand you want. If that's the case, don't get discouraged! The next chapters will help you to communicate your brand while you work on strengthening it.

Step 2
Communicate it

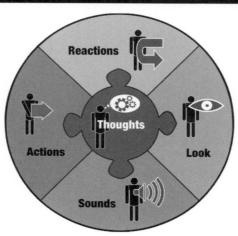

Leadership
Personal Brand Marketing Plan

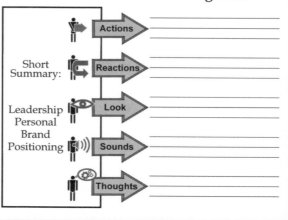

11

Launching Your Leadership Personal Brand

All paths lead to the same goal: to convey to others what we are.

— Pablo Neruda, Chilean poet

Pablo Neruda's above quote is certainly true, especially when it comes to leadership personal brands. Of course, in your case, it's about how you want to be viewed by your Audience. But no matter how brilliant the brand is that you have defined, it will be useless unless you communicate it to others. And you must communicate it consistently. Only then will YOU™ make the leap from a concept in your mind to a perception in the mind of your Audience that is exactly what you want it to be. Then, you and YOU™ will be interchangeable. This is what will help you take control of your career, attain a higher position, achieve the recognition you desire and deserve, and create a better financial future for yourself.

Your Leadership Personal Brand's Coming-Out Party

How do you communicate the leadership personal brand you've worked so hard to define?

Let's turn to successful product brands to see how they communicate to their Target Markets what they want to stand for. Sit back for a moment, and think of one brand that you feel particularly strongly about—a brand that you use regularly and that you have a powerful connection with. How has this particular brand communicated to you what it stands for? How has it made clear to you the elements of its Positioning Statement? How has this brand found its way through your pocketbook and into your heart?

Perhaps you're loyal to Colgate toothpaste because, with regular use, you haven't had a cavity in five years. Or, maybe your brother-in-law come out of a rollover accident without a bruise while driving a Volvo. Do you take your kids to McDonald's because of the Happy Meals and the playgrounds?

What these examples show is that a product brand communicates its positioning to you via what it *does*, not by what it *says* it is. Think about it: You've never seen McDonald's Brand Positioning Statement, and the Brand Manager at Virgin Airlines isn't likely to invite you to dinner in order to show you the definition of Virgin's Brand Character. Instead, it's the *experience* you have with a brand that most communicates its positioning statement.

So, the key to success of any brand is how consistently it communicates what it does. For example, Volvo wouldn't sponsor a demolition derby, but it *would* sponsor a family car safety day. Nike wouldn't support an online computer game contest targeted at teens, but it *would* support a charity marathon. To be consistent in its communications, Volvo will continue to focus on safety in everything it presents to the public, and Nike will regularly communicate its "Just Do It" get-out-there-and-make-it-happen attitude to its sports-loving target market. This kind of consistency is the Holy Grail when it comes to successfully positioning a brand.

It's the same with self-branding. I can show you my Leadership Personal Brand Positioning Statement, and I can tell you that's what I stand for. But the perceptions, thoughts, and feelings you have about me will be based on what I *do*, not on what I say.

The Five Activities That Most Communicate Your Leadership Personal Brand

You know now that your leadership personal brand is communicated by what you *do*. But "what you do" is a pretty big category. After having watched hundreds of people in corporations throughout the world build (or damage) their individual brands at work, I have come to the conclusion that there are five core activities that we all do each and every day that most communicate our leadership personal brands. I really believe these five activities are responsible for 99% of how your Audience perceives, thinks, and feels about YOU™.

Here are the five activities:

Your ... **Actions**

Your ... **Reactions**

Your ... **Look**

Your ... **Sound**

Your ... **Thoughts**

Remember the Leadership Personal Brand Marketing Plan we mentioned at the beginning of the book? Just like successful name brands have full-blown marketing plans to make sure they communicate their messages consistently across TV commercials, magazine ads, sponsored events, the company's website, social media, the brand's packaging, public relations efforts, etc., the five activities we are going to talk about are your own "media" of sorts when it comes to your individual Leadership Personal Brand Marketing Plan. These activities are your way of communicating to your Audience who YOU™ really are.

If you're serious about how you want others to perceive, think, and feel about you as a self-leader or leader of others, you owe it to yourself to keep these five activities top of mind every single day in order to consistently communicate the brand you want for yourself.

Your Leadership Personal Brand Marketing Plan

Let's take a look at the format of our Leadership Personal Brand Marketing Plan. On the left side, you will place a brief summary of your Leadership Personal Brand Positioning Statement. On the right, you'll create a Marketing Plan using each of the five brand communication activities.

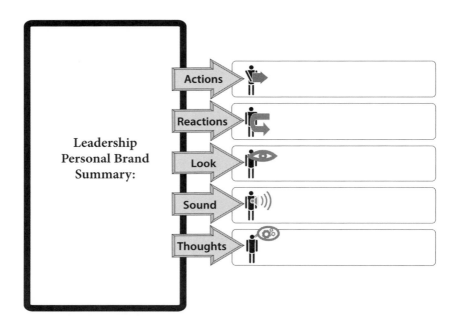

First, you want to summarize your personal brand. Think of your Leadership Personal Brand Summary as "the bottom line"—a short statement that pulls it all together to express the heart of what YOU™ want to stand for.

Take a look at the various elements of your Leadership Personal Brand Positioning Statement, and then sum up the "essence" of the brand you want to communicate. Your summary can come from different parts of your statement, e.g., from your Brand Character, your Unique Strengths, your Desired Identity, your Reasons Why, or a combination of one or more of these elements.

Let's take a look at how our two colleagues, Kathleen and Eric, have summarized their leadership personal brands. This will help you get the idea.

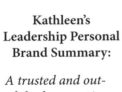

Kathleen's Leadership Personal Brand Summary:

A trusted and out-of-the-box creative team leader who never lets up, never lets the team settle for just "good," but spurs on the entire organization to reach higher: a "champion's champion."

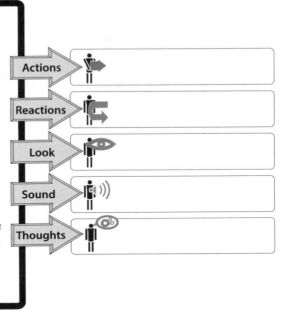

Eric's Leadership Personal Brand Summary:

A "gold standard" setter and achiever, completely reliable and committed to excellence in serving.

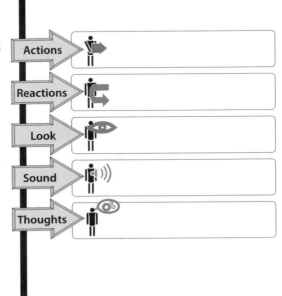

Hopefully, you can see how the summaries of Kathleen and Eric briefly and simply encapsulate what they want their leadership personal brands to stand for.

Now, go ahead and create your own brand summary. At the end of each of the next five chapters, you'll develop ideas about how to leverage the five Marketing Plan activities you do every day to communicate that brand summary.

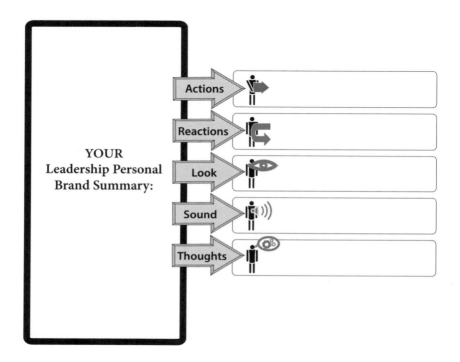

As you make the necessary changes for YOU™ to become a reality, your Audience's perception of you will gradually change. You'll start to see your leadership personal brand in action, and there will be an exciting and profound difference in your image and success on the job. Over time, this can translate to the position, income, and/or the recognition you want.

Communicate it

Actions

12

Leadership Personal Brand Marketing Plan Activity #1: *Actions*

As I grow older, I pay less attention to what men say. I just watch what they do.

— Andrew Carnegie, founder of the U.S. steel industry

The first activity in your Leadership Personal Brand Marketing Plan is your Actions. You may think that all five of the activities mentioned are "actions," but in this case, what I mean by "Actions" are *visually observed behaviors* that others can see and that can influence the way your leadership personal brand is communicated. Think of it as how well you lead yourself—your overall manner as it pertains to self-leadership.

You may not even be aware of some of your Actions, but they can have a huge impact on the way your Audience perceives, thinks, and feels about you.

Think for a second about people you've met. Maybe you recently attended a networking event, and you ran into someone who was unknowingly abrupt, walking away from you without saying goodbye when he or she saw someone else desirable to talk to. What was your impression of that person? Maybe you know someone who is very smart and capable but never looks you in the eye. It can come across as a lack of interest or a lack of confidence. These kinds of Actions influence the way your leadership personal brand is perceived by your Audience.

As a coach, I often "shadow" executives, following them around to observe how they behave in the workplace. Before shadowing, many executives will tell me, "I have an open door policy," meaning that they are always available to team members and that employees can come into the boss's office whenever they want. When I shadow those same executives, though, their office door is often closed, and they aren't communicating with their teams as much or as well as they thought. These executives are unaware of how the action of closing the door to their offices is damaging to their brands as leaders. As an executive coach, it's my job to help them see beyond their blind spots so that they can alter their behaviors and strengthen their brands.

The Actions I'm talking about can be social or directly related to your job. No matter how well you perform in your job, your leadership personal brand will be negatively affected if your Actions put people off. So, how can you take control of your Actions—especially if you're not even conscious of some of them?

See Yourself Through the Eyes of Others

It isn't always easy, but it's important to try to see yourself the way others do. It's critical to know how your Actions "read" from your Audience's perspective. Figuring out which of your Actions might be helping your leadership personal brand—and which ones might be hurting it—is critical to self-branding success.

One of the most important ways to get a handle on your Actions is to be as aware as you can about the signals you send. Keep in mind, of course, that different people interpret Actions in different ways.

For example, let's say Irene works for a boss who is a real stickler about meeting deadlines. That is one of her boss's core Needs— reliability, especially when it comes to deadlines. So, Irene decides that "reliability in meeting deadlines" is one of the key Strengths she will embody in her leadership personal brand. She sets out to communicate this Strength consistently to her boss through her Actions. But just meeting the deadline may or may not communicate her brand the way she wants.

Let's say Irene's boss asks her to turn in a report by Wednesday morning at 8:00 a.m.

- If Irene turns in the report on *Tuesday* morning at 8:00 a.m.—one full day in advance—that's a very different "reliable" brand than …

- If Irene turns in the report on Wednesday morning at 7:59 a.m. —one minute in advance. Yes, she has technically made the deadline, and this is still a "reliable" brand, but that's still a very different "reliable" brand than ...

- If Irene comes running in at 2:00 p.m. on Wednesday afternoon —six hours late—with her report mangled, saying that it slipped out of her briefcase and was trampled in the street. That isn't much of a "reliable" brand at all.

When you assess your Actions, put yourself in the shoes of your Audience. What would you think of someone who gives you a short, vague proposal, as opposed to someone who provides you with a fleshed-out proposal that has a title page and charts that show the advantages of an idea? Or how would you feel about someone who presents you with an excessively long and wordy proposal? Which one of these people would you most likely choose to work with again in the future? Each of them may have the same desired leadership personal brand of "the go-to person for innovative ideas," but each person's Actions will have a big impact on how their desired leadership personal brand is communicated.

Asssessing Your Own Behaviour

There are several ways to discover which of your Actions may need adjustment.

1. Make a video of yourself. Watching yourself can be an eye-opening life-changer! It may not be something you enjoy doing, but it's almost guaranteed to help you see what you need to work on in order to improve the way others perceive you.

2. Ask a close confidante to observe your behavior when you are interacting with your Audience and to give you feedback. Ideally, this confidante should be in a position to watch you without it being too obvious. Make sure you choose someone you trust and who has your best interests at heart.

3. Watch carefully for signals from the people around you. Do they seem relaxed and friendly toward you? If not, what aspects of your behavior might be making people uncomfortable?

4. If you give a presentation at a meeting, ask some attendees to give you feedback afterward. If you see people there you trust, you might even tell them about the work you're doing with your leadership personal brand, and ask them if your Actions supported it or not. While you are at it, ask them what Actions would have helped to communicate your brand even better. Remember the Five Words Exercise? You could even ask attendees what five words they would use to describe you based on the visibly observed self-leadership behaviors you demonstrated during the presentation.

Watch Your Body Language

You may have unknowingly adopted habits that work *against* the brand you want to communicate. Say, for example, that you are in an important meeting, and you suddenly hear an annoying tapping sound. Look around—it may very well be you tapping your foot or a pen against a table. Most people are completely unaware of the unconscious signals they send to others simply by how they move. If you're exhibiting nervous Actions that you are not even aware of, begin to notice them in order to get a handle on your excitement or anxiety.

The body language you communicate may make you appear as if you lack confidence. Here are some additional "nervous" body language Actions to watch for:

- Biting your nails

- Drumming your fingers on the table

- Crossing your legs and swinging your foot up and down repeatedly

- Blinking rapidly (which can also be a sign that you are lying—a real watch-out!)

- Gripping the arms of your chair

- Fidgeting. If you have a habit of shifting in your seat, playing with your pen, etc., consciously work toward staying as still as you can.

- Using your hands too much when you speak. According to psychologists who have studied body language, confident people don't feel the need to prove their points by gesturing too much.

- Letting your eyes wander while others are speaking. If your eyes *do* wander, the person talking may get the idea that you're not interested in what he or she is saying.

Maintain "open" body language that will communicate friendliness. Here are some open body language tips:

- If you want someone to know you're interested in what he or she is saying, lean forward slightly.

- If you want to show sincerity when making a point, touch your palm to your chest as you speak.

- Avoid folding your arms across your chest because it communicates that you're closing yourself off.

- Avoid putting your hands into your pants pockets because that can be interpreted as protectiveness.

- Men, when you first walk into a room, have your suit jacket buttoned, but feel free to unbutton it when you sit down. Not only will this keep your jacket from bunching up, but it will send a signal that you are receptive.

- What about when you're sitting? Experts say it's fine to cross your legs comfortably (as long as you don't swing your foot up and down).

- Don't lean far back in your chair or clasp your hands behind your head while you're sitting. This conveys an attitude that's too casual and may even come across as over-confident or cocky.

- If you're sitting at a table, resting your elbows on the table with the fingertips of both of your hands touching is considered an expression of calm self-confidence.

Observe the body language of people you feel drawn to. What are they doing that makes them so likeable? On the other hand, what Actions do you see in people who don't come across as all that likeable or approachable? This is yet another reason why making a video of yourself can be so valuable. You may notice yourself unconsciously doing something that you've seen unapproachable people do. By discovering it now, you can fix it before it derails your brand.

Your Leadership Personal Brand Marketing Plan

As you reflect on your Actions, what do you think you should work on most as you consider how to effectively communicate your brand? With that in mind, it's time to pull together the Action portion of your Leadership Personal Brand Marketing Plan. To help you, Kathleen and Eric have done the same. Review what they've written, then complete the Actions portion of your own Marketing Plan.

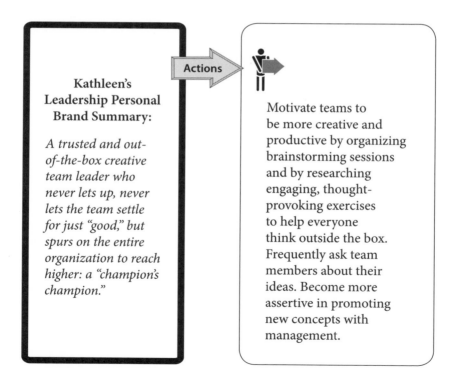

Kathleen's Leadership Personal Brand Summary:

A trusted and out-of-the-box creative team leader who never lets up, never lets the team settle for just "good," but spurs on the entire organization to reach higher: a "champion's champion."

Actions

Motivate teams to be more creative and productive by organizing brainstorming sessions and by researching engaging, thought-provoking exercises to help everyone think outside the box. Frequently ask team members about their ideas. Become more assertive in promoting new concepts with management.

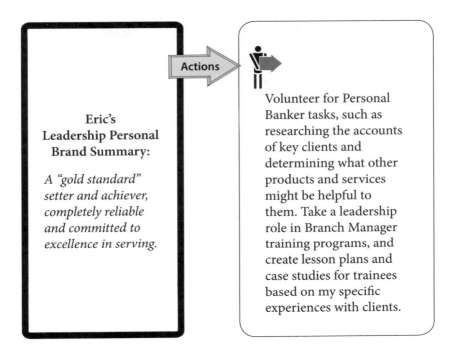

Eric's
Leadership Personal Brand Summary:

A "gold standard" setter and achiever, completely reliable and committed to excellence in serving.

Actions

Volunteer for Personal Banker tasks, such as researching the accounts of key clients and determining what other products and services might be helpful to them. Take a leadership role in Branch Manager training programs, and create lesson plans and case studies for trainees based on my specific experiences with clients.

Now that you've seen how Kathleen and Eric will use their Actions to market their leadership personal brands, you should have an idea of what Actions you can take to communicate YOU™. What Actions do you need to work on in order to make your desired brand a reality in the mind of your Audience?

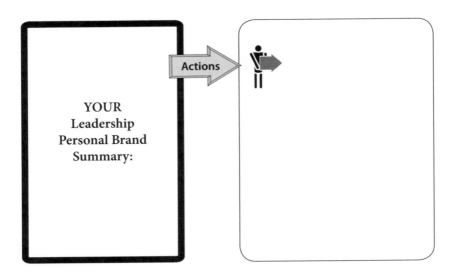

YOUR Leadership Personal Brand Summary:

Actions

Communicate it

Step 2

13

Leadership Personal Brand Marketing Plan Activity #2: *Reactions*

It's not the situation. It's your reaction to the situation.
— Robert Conklin, author

Remember when former U.S. President Bill Clinton was proven to have lied under oath? When he was accused of sexual misconduct in the White House, at first he vehemently denied what was later proven to be true. A few years after that, when President Clinton published his memoir, he addressed the situation quite differently and told the truth, explaining that it was a mistake. So, his first Reaction when faced with a tough challenge was to lie. His second Reaction was to explain it as a personal failure. Ultimately, he recovered well from the entire affair (every pun intended!), but it's a great lesson in how important Reactions can be and the kind of impact your Reactions can have on your own individual brand.

Let's face it, when things are going great, it's easy to stay consistent with your desired brand. It's when things *don't* go well that you may find it hard to maintain the brand you are aiming for. Most of us face our biggest leadership personal brand Reaction challenges when we're nervous or under pressure. If you want to see others' true leadership personal brand emerge, watch them react to a difficult situation. That's because how you react to events and circumstances can make or break your brand. A negative knee-jerk Reaction to a situation can seriously undermine your brand and prevent you from reaching your full potential.

The Reactions I'm talking about here are Reactions that you can see, read, or hear—how you might respond to an unexpected challenge. (Your Reactions can also take the form of negative Thought Reactions, but that's not the focus of this particular chapter. We'll get to that subject later on.) The Reactions you have that can be seen, read, or heard will definitely influence the way your Audience perceives, thinks, and feels about YOU™.

The bottom line is this: The way you react to situations is a "torture test" for sticking to and communicating your leadership personal brand. How do YOU™ typically react?

Whose Emotions Are These Anyway?

Have you ever heard the phrase, "You can't always control what happens to you, but you *can* control how you react to it?" I'm not sure who originally coined that phrase, but I couldn't agree more. We often say, "He made me feel bad about my work," or "Her comments about my presentation made me so angry!" The truth is that someone else's Actions may push a button that could impact your emotions, but only *you* are responsible for how you react. No one can "make" you feel anything. You are in charge, so how you react is a choice you make. It's up to you to transform your Reactions. I'm talking about mastering self-control, an important element of self-leadership.

Think about how you might typically react to something unpleasant that happens. Maybe an unexpected urgent request arrived two minutes before you were leaving the office, or your boss sent you an e-mail reprimanding you for something you didn't do. If you're like most people, your automatic Reaction probably comes instinctually—from your "gut"—without much conscious thought.

An automatic Reaction like that may actually be based on a habit you've developed over time. Sometimes, without even realizing it, a comment someone makes can bring up a past negative situation from years ago that sends you into emotional overdrive. Or maybe you've conditioned yourself to react in a certain way because that's the way you saw your mother or father respond when bad things happened. You might have had a boss for a long time who went on a tirade if you didn't respond immediately to a question or an incident. So, your negative Reactions may just be ingrained learned habits in disguise.

Taking Control

For many of us, learning to suppress old Reaction habits and replace them with new, more positive habits can be challenging. In fact, learning to control emotions can be a life-long lesson. But the truth is that knee-jerk Reactions almost always lead to difficulties, and they'll do little to further your brand. In fact, they will most often make things worse for you in the long run.

Here's an example: Connie was trying to finalize multiple elements (brochures, in-store point of purchase materials, etc.) for an important promotion her company was running. The project was already two days late getting to the printer. That was not the fault of the small, local design team that Connie had hired to do the job. It was Connie's fault, driven mainly by poor time management, and she was really feeling the pressure. Fortunately, the design team had always delivered for her in the past, so she had no doubt they would do all they could to help her this time, too.

When Connie last talked with the design team, she was promised that the materials would be sent no later than noon the next day. The following morning, however, Connie noticed a small mistake that she had overlooked and called the printer in a panic to tell them about it so that they could fix it at the last minute. There was no response. In fact, the answering machine said the entire design company was closed for the day!

Connie was furious and reacted immediately by leaving a message on the company's voicemail, criticizing the designer and saying that this would be the last time she would ever work with them. Fifteen minutes later, the phone rang, and it was the head of the design firm. He explained that they had closed the office that morning in order to put "all hands on deck" toward getting the design work Connie needed completed by her noon deadline. From his tone, Connie could tell that he had heard the remarks she had left on the answering machine. She was embarrassed and apologized profusely, but from then on, the relationship was never the same. Connie's Reaction ended up damaging a previously great working relationship.

Based on my many years of shadowing executives, I've learned that knee-jerk Reactions rarely strengthen leadership personal brand images.

The Art of Calming Yourself Down

Here are a couple of fast and easy techniques to help you release negative emotions and get back to a place of equilibrium. The more you practice them, the faster they will help you take control of your Reactions and protect your leadership brand.

Deep breathing. When you have a negative Reaction to an incident, your body reacts with faster heartbeats and shallow breathing. This is a natural fight-or-flight response, but taking deep breaths can counteract that. Practice breathing from your diaphragm, inhaling deeply, and exhaling slowly.

Positive self-talk. When you feel angry or upset, psychologists say that one of the best ways to get yourself into a better emotional state of mind is to talk yourself out of it. You may not be able to fully resolve the emotion right away, but you can take the edge off of it in order to keep your Reactions in check.

For example, let's consider this scenario: A co-worker tells you that a colleague has spoken negatively about you to your boss without you knowing about it. You could react by yelling at the colleague, or you could react by storming into your boss's office. But since you don't know yet if the incident actually occurred, you could end up doing a lot of harm for no good reason.

Instead, practice self-talk to manage your emotions and get back to the *facts,* e.g., what you really know to be true. For example, you don't know what was said or what impact it had, if any, on your boss's opinion of you. You could remind yourself that you have a good relationship with your boss, and that one person's opinion is unlikely to change your image within the company. You could tell yourself that even if the worst comes to pass, you will present yourself professionally and with dignity. Even if you decide to go to your boss and ask what took place, your self-talk will help you enter that office calmly and with confidence.

Get a Grip on Your Leadership Personal Brand

Below are a few ideas to help you learn to control your knee-jerk Reactions in a way that shows your self-leadership and aligns with the brand you want for yourself at work. The first three are the most common types of visible Reactions you're likely to show, and the fourth has to do with written and vocal Reactions.

Do these sound familiar to you? I know I've personally experienced all of these Reactions at some point.

1. **Facial Reactions.** Do you wear your heart on your sleeve … or, rather, on your face? If you are someone who tends to be transparent—baring your feelings and thoughts on your face for all to see—try practicing your "poker face" in the mirror. Or, ask a friend/trusted colleague to watch you and share their perspective on your facial reactions. The more you are aware of your facial reactions and the more you practice, the better you'll be able to keep your cool in difficult on-the-job situations.

2. **Verbal Reactions.** If you tend to become easily angry or verbally defensive when an unexpected negative situation arises, ask for a break. The most effective tool I've seen good brand builders use for this problem is to take five to ten minutes to cool off and gather their thoughts before responding. People will respect you more for it. Simply say, "I need to take a few minutes to collect my thoughts, and then I'll get back to you." The key is to "know thyself" and do what *you* need in order to avoid a damaging Reaction.

   Sometimes, the less said, the better. In fact, the best Reaction may simply be to remain quiet. The *absence* of a verbal Reaction can communicate strength and conviction. Learn to be comfortable with silence when it's appropriate, and it could work to your benefit.

3. **Physical Reactions.** Many people respond to negative situations with physical reactions like sweaty palms or turning red in the face. Some people may tap a pen or foot repeatedly to ease the tension. If you're prone to any of these Reactions, learn to calm yourself internally with self-talk or deep breathing. Research shows that deep breathing not only slows your heartbeat, but it also affects your neurological system, altering your body

chemistry. You may even find the warmth that comes from placing the palms of your hands over your lower belly to be calming in stressful situations, serving as a "reset button" for your body.

4. **Telephone and E-mail Reactions.** Never respond on the phone or in an e-mail in a way that you wouldn't respond if you were face-to-face. If someone is rude to you on the phone or in an e-mail, take a deep breath and count to five in your head. While this person may not even be your Audience, he or she could easily make negative remarks about you to someone who *is* your Audience or who knows your Audience well. In other words, your leadership personal brand is "on" all the time. So, it simply isn't worth it to have a knee-jerk response to someone who might just be having a bad day. Remember the brand you are working to communicate, and pick your battles carefully. The satisfaction of telling someone off for a petty comment is much less than the satisfaction of a great personal brand that takes your career to new heights.

Here are some tips for keeping these kinds of Reactions under control:

Prepare! Be ready with your Reactions *before* a crisis happens. How do you do this? Start by making a list of the many ways someone with your leadership personal brand would react in different situations. What incidents have you encountered in your work life, and how would someone with your brand respond to those? What facial Reactions, physical Reactions, body stance, etc. would this person exhibit? How would this person communicate his or her brand via the way he or she reacts?

For example, let's look at Eric's Leadership Personal Brand Summary statement. He's our Associate Branch Manager at Hudson International Bank, and you will remember that his leadership personal brand is: "A 'gold standard' setter and achiever, completely reliable and committed to excellence in serving." How would someone with this brand react if a customer approached him, upset about a problem that was clearly the customer's fault? Would he point out that she had made the mistake herself, or would he, as someone committed to excellence in serving, take a deep breath, and resolve the problem with tact and courtesy?

Exploring different scenarios and Reactions based on the brand you want to communicate will give you a roadmap for dealing with any number of situations that may come up at work. You'll be able to quickly move yourself beyond your gut Reaction because you will have learned to react instinctively with the thought, "This is the type of situation in which someone with my leadership personal brand would respond by focusing on what's going well with the team." When something unexpected comes your way, you'll be more confident since you've prepared how to react.

Use every experience to improve. When things don't go exactly as you planned, don't be too hard on yourself. Just focus on what you can improve in the future. None of us is perfect, but the key is to learn from mistakes, figure out what you would do better the next time, and add it to your Marketing Plan as something to work on.

When You Think You Might React Negatively...

- Ask yourself immediately and honestly: What is the benefit of having a negative knee-jerk Reaction? What result is that likely to bring you other than the temporary satisfaction of expressing your immediate emotional response? Remind yourself that you can release your emotions in private, and that knee-jerk Reactions will only entrench you deeper in the image you already have rather than the brand you are trying to build for yourself. Keep your eyes on the prize of your desired leadership personal brand, and remember that change takes time and discipline.

- Use self-talk to remind yourself of the brand you are trying to communicate. Over and over in your mind, repeat the key characteristics you want to convey. Remember that no matter how justified you may feel in saying something in anger, the important thing is to stay focused on the brand you want to communicate. Keep your Leadership Personal Brand Summary in a prominent place where you can be constantly reminded of what you're working toward.

- Set yourself up for success in advance. For example, if you expect a less-than-receptive response to a presentation you're preparing to make to your Audience, remember that *environment* can have a lot to do with how others react. Is the room too hot or too cold?

Are people cramped for space? Would it be better to move to a larger room? Create the best possible environment to keep you and everyone else focused and positive.

- Remember that your Reactions may impact everyone near you and not just your specific Audience. Here's an example: Richard took a job as the Head of Accounting in a new firm—a job he had wanted for a long time. Shortly after he took the position, he was in his office with his door closed, having a telephone discussion with the company's key banking contact. Unfortunately, the conversation wasn't going well, and Richard got so frustrated that he started yelling at the banker. Richard didn't realize it, but his entire accounting team could hear him screaming through the closed door. When he came out of his office, his staff stared at him with concerned looks on their faces. He told me later that their faces seemed to be communicating the question, "Am *I* next?"

Avoid Regrets

If you're like me, you can think of situations you wish you could relive, reacting in a different way that wouldn't make you cringe when you think back on them later. So, one more way to gain better control over your Reactions is to think about how you want to remember experiences in the future. To avoid regrets, how could you react in a way that you would be proud to reflect on later?

When I'm on the verge of reacting negatively, I've found it helpful to take a moment and ask myself: "Is this really as bad as I think it is?" Once the initial flood of emotion passes, I can better separate my emotions from the situation and see things more clearly. So, overreacting will most likely just lead to a regretful memory, especially if it seriously undermines your leadership personal brand in the process. Why add to your list of unpleasant memories?

Putting Your Reactions into Action

Now, let's check in on Kathleen and Eric to see how they plan to manage their Reactions as part of their Leadership Personal Brand Marketing Plans.

Kathleen's Leadership Personal Brand Summary:

A trusted and out-of-the-box creative team leader who never lets up, never lets the team settle for just "good," but spurs on the entire organization to reach higher: a "champion's champion."

Reactions

Prepare a list of Reactions for when superiors don't accept ideas right away. Work on staying calm when Bruce does his usual "put-down" of new concepts. When appropriate, don't be afraid to respond with silence instead of jumping in and starting to talk.

Eric's Leadership Personal Brand Summary:

A "gold standard" setter and achiever, completely reliable and committed to excellence in serving.

Reactions

Practice positive self-talk in difficult situations with the Branch Manager, reminding myself not to take her stress personally; prepare and anticipate various applicable Reactions for frustrated customers in order to keep my cool.

Okay, now, it's your turn. How do your Reactions need adjustment in order to consistently communicate your leadership personal brand?

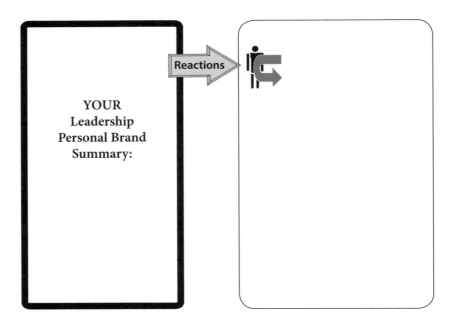

Communicate it

Look

14

Leadership Personal Brand Marketing Plan Activity #3: *Look*

Never trust a skinny chef.

— Anonymous

I t's a proven cold, hard reality that people judge you first and foremost based on the way you look, from head to toe. We all do it—it's simply human nature. In fact, research shows that first impressions are made within the first three to seven seconds of meeting someone.

I can hear you out there saying, "But I don't have a movie star face or body . . . what can I do about that?" Hey, I'm no beauty queen myself, and no one expects you to be either. It's not about being gorgeous; it's about presenting the best possible Look for *your* leadership personal brand.

You've probably heard the old adage: "You never get a second chance to make a first impression." That is true, but it doesn't mean that you won't get a chance to make a *second* impression that could change the first impression someone has of you. Nonetheless, no matter how you slice it, that original image can be a tough one to undo. It takes hard work to get others to change their initial impression of you since that first leadership personal brand image happens so quickly and unconsciously. So, creating the best Look for your leadership personal brand will help you come across as the YOU™ that you want your Audience to see.

The Packaged YOU™

Think of your Look as your leadership personal brand "packaging." Just like a bottle that holds shampoo has been designed with a certain brand image in mind, so your Look communicates a whole host of things about YOU™, too. Just from the way you look, your Audience will form opinions about your values, your attitudes, your worth, who you are, what you stand for, and what you have to offer.

Big companies put a lot of time and money into developing a brand's package design because they know how important the "outside" is to an overall brand image. They know that a brand's Character comes through loud and clear through packaging, and they know that Character has a lot to do with how well that brand actually sells.

If you think about it, doesn't a brand's packaging help you make choices when you are shopping? Imagine yourself standing in a supermarket aisle, and you have to choose between two brands that you don't know much about. All other things being equal, if you're like most people, you will most likely choose the brand with the packaging you like the best.

Your Audience looks at the trademarked YOU™ the same way.

I know that you cannot control every aspect of your Look. And I'm definitely not suggesting you head for a plastic surgeon's office! The key is simply to take charge of those aspects of your Look that *are* in your control. You are the Brand Manager of YOU™, and it's your job to make sure your "packaging" sets you up to make a great impression at first glance and beyond.

Watch Out!

Many people have a misperception that personal branding is all about how you Look—your hairstyle, how you dress, whether or not you're wearing the "right" tie or the appropriate length of skirt, etc. But trying to communicate a great brand for yourself by focusing only on how you look is just scratching the surface of who YOU™ really are.

Don't get me wrong—your Look *is* an important element of your individual brand, and it definitely plays a big part in helping to communicate YOU™. (I wouldn't have devoted an entire chapter to it if it didn't.) But hopefully, you realize by now that your brand as a leader is communicated by so much more than just the way you look.

Learning to Look Like YOU™

Your Look is not necessarily about being beautiful or handsome. It's about projecting to the world your brand as you've defined it. It's about embodying the brand that you want to communicate. Always remember that when you make decisions about your Look. To help you with that, here is a checklist of some key aspects of your Look to keep in mind as you work on communicating YOU™. Let's work from your head down to your toes—and beyond.

Your Hair. Unless your leadership personal brand is "funky rock star," keep this in mind: Frequent, drastic changes to your hairstyle might not convey the best brand image at work. When I was very young, I learned the hard way that overnight changes to my hair could wreak havoc with my brand. I was in my first job right out of college, and I showed up one morning with a wildly curly perm (think Orphan Annie). I was 22, so I thought it was fun and interesting, but the rest of the team thought otherwise. (Of course, when I look at photos of me with that hairstyle now, I cringe...) I hadn't been with the company very long, so suddenly, everyone was looking at me like, "What's she going to do next?" Instead of communicating a brand of stability, which was really at the core of what I was trying to establish since it was early in my career, I had accidentally communicated a brand of *unpredictability*. This didn't fly because my boss/Audience at that time was a more traditional male in his mid-40s. Oops!

The moral of this story is that changing your appearance a lot may not say what you want about your willingness to stay the course in your job. Others may think that, if you are unpredictable and do things like drastically changing your hair, you will suddenly not show up at work one day. Will you quit with a week's notice in order to move to Tasmania? Okay, I'm exaggerating here, but you get the point.

At work, your Audience—like all of us—has a lot of things to worry about and manage, such as organizational changes, technology changes, personnel changes, etc. And all of that change can cause stress. So, why add more change and stress to the environment by constantly revising and updating the way you look? It can freak people out! Like it or not, almost everyone likes to work with people they know they can depend on. So, it's better to avoid sending signals that could give the impression you have a fly-by-night personality. You don't want to be remembered for your hairstyle. It's your values, your strengths, and your passions that you want to shine through instead.

That said, if your leadership personal brand is "raucously creative," go for the hair changes! For the rest of us, drastic changes may not be such a good idea.

Your Skin. You may be thinking, "My skin? What the heck does my skin have to do with my brand?" Well, let's face it: Your skin is one of the most visible parts of your physical appearance, and it can actually say a lot about how well you take care of yourself. I can hear you saying, "Unfair! I wasn't blessed with flawless skin." Well, join the sizable club—most of us weren't. You don't have to have perfect skin; you just need to do the best with what you have. Simply learn what your skin needs in order to look as healthy as possible … and this goes for men, too.

> ➤ *For the Men.* More and more attention is being paid to how well men take care of themselves. In recent times, dozens of new male skincare products have been introduced into the market for a reason. So, guys, the (skincare) bar is rising. Step up to the plate, and check out a product or two. This means shaving daily—sorry!—and/or trimming your facial hair regularly (assuming your brand isn't Colin Farrell-tough-boy, of course).

> ➤ *For the Women.* When men get older, their lines and wrinkles can look more "sophisticated," but when women age, they sometimes find themselves relegated to the back office. How's that for a harsh reality? It's an unfair truth that men seem to be able to get away with much more as their skin ages. It is what it is—at least for now. So, women, just accept that having younger-looking skin requires a bit more work. Great leadership personal brand builders do.

Here's another startling reality: Research reveals that women who wear makeup earn 20% to 30% more money than those who don't. I strongly recommend that all women ignore this advice—unless, of course, you want to make more money! If you don't like to wear makeup, that's fine—just keep it light and simple. Too much is worse than too little, but too little will do nothing to help your leadership personal brand (or your pocketbook).

Lastly, if you haven't yet heard about the damage that UV rays do to your skin, what rock have you been living under!? All kidding aside, those nasty statistics are true. Some family members of mine have suffered from serious skin cancers, so I know first-hand that it's no laughing matter. Even if your brand is about being rugged, too much time in the sun without sunscreen will eventually catch up with you.

Your Smile. According to facial-expression expert Paul Ekman, a Professor Emeritus of Psychology at the University of California-San Francisco, a smile can be seen from 30 meters away and immediately indicates that the person smiling has "benign intentions." So, don't be afraid to smile when it's appropriate—especially when you meet someone for the first time. A natural, comfortable smile that says, "I'm confident, I'm self-assured, and I'm friendly" can go miles (or at least 30 meters) toward communicating the personal brand image you want.

Your Body. Another tried-and-true piece of advice is to get regular exercise. How many times have you heard this one? But many medical studies have proven that exercise makes you *look* better because it makes you healthier. Here's what else exercise has been proven to do:

- Make you feel better.
- Help your clothes fit better.
- Increase your blood circulation, which improves the color of your skin.
- Make you sleep better, which reduces dark eye circles and eye bags.

All of that is hard to refute, so get out there and exercise. The healthier you look, the better impression you'll make on your Audience. Doesn't your leadership personal brand deserve a jog around the park?

Your Posture. I can still hear my mother telling me: "Watch your posture! Stand up straight!" At the time, I didn't know what a strong personal brand secret she was sharing, but now I know she was right. Great leadership personal brand builders recognize what body language experts have said for years: Powerful self-confidence is communicated by holding your shoulders erect and not slumping. Look straight ahead as you walk, not down, in order to convey self-assurance.

The same is true when you're sitting in a chair: Don't slouch. If you're wearing a suit jacket, tuck the bottom of it underneath you as you sit down so that it doesn't ride up around your neck. A suit jacket looks better buttoned when you're standing, but if it's buttoned while you're sitting, it will bunch up. Women can have this problem, too.

Ladies, if you're planning on wearing a skirt, check to make sure it doesn't move up too high on your thighs when you sit down. How about your blouse? Does it gape open when you sit? Try it beforehand to check yourself in a mirror.

Your Clothes. The trend in quite a few developed countries during the last decade and a half has been toward casual wear in offices. Yet, *USA Today* reported that, during that same period of time, sexual harassment lawsuits in corporate America skyrocketed. "Why?" the article asked. The theory is that people are dressing so casually in the office—the same way they might dress to go bar-hopping, for example—that their behavior in the office begins to mimic their behavior in bars. So, how we dress sends signals to ourselves and to those around us about what is and what isn't proper behavior. Don't underestimate its importance.

Actors will often tell you that they can immediately step into character when they're given the right costume. So, how you dress not only influences the way others perceive you, but it will likely impact how you perceive *yourself*, too, and therefore, how you act. And you already know how important your Actions are when it comes to communicating your brand to others.

Think of it this way: If you want to "act" professionally, you need to wear the right costume for the play you're in. As a smart leadership personal brand builder, you want to make sure that everything you wear communicates your brand and how YOU™ want to be perceived on the job.

Here are some other things to consider when choosing a wardrobe for YOU™:

- Invest in *quality* clothes. Spend less time worrying about the latest fashion, which can sometimes be too over-the-top for anything but the fashion industry anyway. Even if your budget isn't quite at a point where you can have a full wardrobe that's just perfect for your brand, spend the extra time and money to get some good quality items. People tend to pay more attention to quality than quantity anyway.

- Make sure your clothes are clean—not worn, torn, or missing buttons. Here is a related personal story: When I managed laundry brands at Procter & Gamble, all I had to do was say that I worked in detergents, and everyone inevitably looked immediately at … you guessed it … my clothes. Remember our skinny chef from the opening quote of this chapter? It was the same thing with me and the clothes I wore when I worked on detergent brands. People expected that what I wore would be in tip-top shape because of my job. Talk about pressure! So, I started paying more attention to making sure my clothing could pass a spot inspection. It actually turned out to be a good lesson in leadership personal brand building. My clothes and I represented the Cheer and Ariel brands back then just as you represent the "YOU™ brand" in *your* workplace now. You owe it to your individual brand to do YOU™ justice via the clothes you wear.

- Take some time to look at your clothes objectively from an outsider's perspective. What does your wardrobe say about YOU™? If you find it hard to be objective, ask a trusted friend or even an image consultant to give you an opinion. Then, be sure to check your clothes for frayed hems, rips, stains, and hanging threads. Do you have a skirt or jacket that is well past its wear-out date? If so, wouldn't you feel better letting those items go? Do it for YOU™.

Your Accessories. When it comes to accessories, there are two key principles that great personal branders follow: First, aim for quality, not quantity. Choose your accessories carefully, and don't overdo it. Accessories (belts, ties, cufflinks, scarves, jewelry, etc.) are just that—accessories. This means that they're supposed to *add* to what you're wearing—not overpower your Look.

Second, check to see that your accessories are consistent with what YOU™ want to stand for and what your Audience will find appropriate. If your brand is "reliable with the occasional surprising edge," then, by all means go ahead and clip a funny pin on your jacket lapel, or wear a bold tie. The key is to make sure your accessories are helping to communicate your leadership personal brand, not to distract from it.

Your Hands. Your hands are seen a lot more than you may realize. One moment, you're using your hand to reference what you've written on a flip chart. The next moment, you're pointing your finger at a report while sitting across from your boss at her desk, and the next, you're flagging down a taxi with a client. Unless you're a factory worker, if your fingernails are ragged or dirty, or the skin on your hands is dry and scaly, your hands may just be pointing to the wrong leadership personal brand impression.

So, don't underestimate the importance of grooming your hands— and that goes for both men and women. More and more, men are expected to have clean, well-groomed hands and fingernails. If you're not already scheduling manicures as part of the proper care and feeding of your leadership personal brand, how about starting now?

Your Shoes. I've heard it said that your shoes reveal the true you, and I have to admit: When I was single, a man's shoes were often one of the first things I noticed. Were his shoes clean? Scuffed? Shined? Out of style? Cheap? I promise you that I'm not one of those people who are obsessed with shoes, but I honestly felt like I could judge if a guy was right for me based on his shoes. (And, by the way, I ended up with an Allen Edmonds guy through and through.)

Shoes can and do send a strong signal about your leadership personal brand. So, stop for a second and look down—what's on your feet right now? Does what you see represent the brand you want? Take a look at the shoes in your closet, and make sure the "shoe represents YOU™."

Extensions of YOU™

When it comes to your Look, I'm not just talking about your physical self or your wardrobe. How you treat anything else at work for which you are responsible reflects your brand as a leader as well.

Your Desk. What does your desk say about who you are? Is it a mess with stacks of papers, old memos, books, and magazines? Or is it tidy and organized? What brand Character does your desk's condition communicate? Is it consistent with the brand you want?

Your Office / Work Area. Your work environment consists of more than just your desk. Photographs or paintings on your wall, the furniture, and anything else you keep there is also a part of your brand. Look at your office objectively. "Who" do you see there? If you didn't know whose office it belonged to, what would you think about this person? Is this what you want others to perceive, think, and feel about YOU™?

Your "Written" Look. When you write e-mails or create memos, reports, presentations, and charts, do they *look* attractive? Are they well laid out so that the important information is easy to find? How well does your "written look" represent YOU™?

Your "Look" on the Internet

Your Look on the Internet could hurt your leadership personal brand in a number of serious ways. There are countless stories in the press about people who have been fired for what they posted on social media. Here are a few examples:

- A college student who was studying to be a teacher posted a photo of herself holding a cup with the words "Drunken Pirate" written on it. That was enough for the dean of her university to deny her a teaching degree. She filed a lawsuit against the university, but lost.

- A bank employee called in sick to say that she was unable to work in front of a computer. When her employer found her to be on Facebook from home, she was fired.

- Virgin Atlantic has taken disciplinary action against flight attendants who post negative comments about passengers on Facebook or Twitter.

So, think twice before posting those wild photos from last year's Mardi Gras on your Facebook page. If you blog, use Twitter, Google+, Instagram, LinkedIn, or any other social networks, pay very close attention to what you share. Never post anything without first asking yourself: "Is this something that someone with my desired leadership personal brand would post for all to see?" Avoid negative comments about other people (especially clients or people at work), and steer away from profanity, strong controversial opinions about politics, or potentially embarrassing personal information about you or anyone else. Remember: Privacy is virtually nonexistent on the Internet. As soon as you post them, your words are "out there," and you may unconsciously damage your leadership personal brand faster than you can click your mouse.

You've Got the "Look"

The bottom line is that there are many aspects of your Look that you can control, and you can have fun with turning the look of "you" into the Look of "YOU™." But don't just dress for your brand on special occasions. Think about it: You would make sure you looked your best for a big presentation for a visiting VIP, so why not pretend that every day involves a big presentation or a meeting with an important visitor? You can make every day your "best-Look-consistent-with-my-leadership-personal-brand day." You'll feel good about yourself, and you'll know that you're being consistent with your desired brand. Plus, you never know when you might be asked to give a spur-of-the-moment presentation to a VIP anyway.

The YOU™ Collage

Your Look and your leadership personal brand should go hand in hand, so go back and review your Brand Character statement. In that section of your Leadership Personal Brand Positioning Statement, you should have five or six descriptive words and/or a narrative sentence that describes your Character. Keeping those words or that narrative in mind, leaf through magazines and newspapers, and cut out pictures and images that you believe best represent those words. You might cut out a photo of a certain type of clothing, a well-manicured hand, a particular hairstyle, a specific pair of shoes, etc.—anything you believe conveys the look you want for YOU™.

Next, find some photos of you—or better yet, take photos of yourself dressed like you think someone with your desired brand would dress—and place them side by side next to the magazine pictures you found. Compare the two. Do you see similar "branding" coming through in your own photos as compared to what you see in the magazine pictures that you cut out? If not, where are you most off track from your desired brand image? Where are you spot-on? Where can you make adjustments? What one or two aspects of your Look could you change that would make the biggest difference in how YOU™ are perceived? Work on making changes to your Look until you more closely match what you liked in those magazine photos.

Your "Look" Marketing Plan

When you sit back and think about your current leadership personal brand image from a Look standpoint, in what ways are you doing well? Where might you be falling short? What will help your Look match the brand that you want to communicate?

To get some different perspectives on this, let's look at how Kathleen and Eric plan to make sure their Looks are in line with their leadership personal brands.

Kathleen's Leadership Personal Brand Summary:

A trusted and out-of-the-box creative team leader who never lets up, never lets the team settle for just "good," but spurs on the entire organization to reach higher: a "champion's champion."

Redecorate office to reflect creative out-of-the-box personal brand. Find new artwork that's cutting edge. Invest in new desk accessories that are modern yet professional.

Eric's Leadership Personal Brand Summary:

A "gold standard" setter and achiever, completely reliable and committed to excellence in serving.

Take better care of my skin and hands—they're in front of customers all the time. Keep nails in shape by having a basic manicure the last Thursday evening of every month. Invest in odorless hand lotion to keep hands from getting so rough due to working with documents and papers all day long.

Now, it's your turn. What is your Look Marketing Plan? What steps will you take to get your Look more in line with the way you want your Audience to perceive, think, and feel about YOU™?

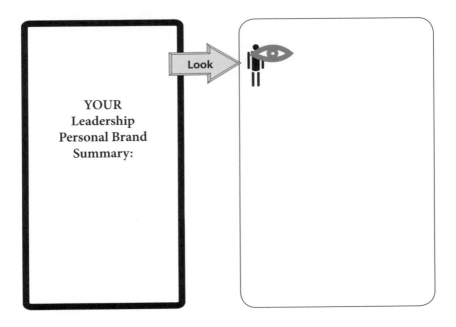

Communicate it

Sound

Step 2

15

Leadership Personal Brand Marketing Plan Activity #4: *Sound*

Sound gives life to our words just as well as the images they conjure up; and the sound is there, whether or not we read them aloud.

— A. A. Patawaran, author

For our purposes, your Sound is not only *what* you say, but *how* you say it. If your voice undermines your leadership personal brand the minute you open your mouth, what you actually say will be less important. So, like your Look, your Sound can create an immediate first impression that has the potential to make or break your brand.

Just how important is the way you sound? Think about it: Sounds impact us often without even realizing it. Maybe it's the sound of a door slamming, a strong wind howling in the middle of the night, a gun firing, a chime swaying in the breeze, or waves crashing onto the beach. Many sounds—not just music—absolutely have the power to influence us.

Are You In Control?

Your voice can carry enormous brand power for you. But just like your Look, there are parts of your Sound that you have control over and parts of it that are outside of your control. The good news is: There are many things about your Sound that you absolutely can—and should—work on in an effort to strengthen your brand as a leader.

Pace. Do you speak too quickly or too slowly? Either extreme can be a problem.

- If you speak too quickly, you may come across as impatient, nervous, or in a rush. Others will likely have trouble keeping up with you, and they may simply stop trying to understand you—a sure sign that communication has broken down.

  Take a cue from U.S. television ads for prescription drugs. After the announcer shares the information that the drug company *wants* you to hear—in a patient "explaining" voice—the announcer will suddenly speed up to an unbelievably fast pace when it comes time to share the drug's side effects, speaking-as-if-there-are-no-spaces-between-words. This information is required by law, but the advertisers speed it up hoping that you will tune it out and/or miss it entirely.

- If you speak too slowly, on the other hand, people will also most likely get tired, impatient, and bored. Here's a helpful clue: If you find that others often finish your sentences or jump in to figure out what you're trying to say next, it might be a sign that you are talking too slowly.

Not sure if your vocal pace is communicating your leadership brand the way you want? Record your voice and listen to it, or ask some friends to tell you if you speak too slowly or too quickly.

Pitch. While you can't change the voice you were given, you *can* alter the pitch. An overly high or low voice can really turn people off. I once had an office assistant who was a great administrator, but her voice—particularly on the phone—was always at a constant, very high pitch. It was so high that a few clients even complained to me that it was uncomfortable to listen to this assistant on the phone. So, I began working with her to help bring down her pitch. We tried a few approaches, but the one that finally worked was for her to pretend that she was a big, burly sumo wrestler with a deep voice—very funny considering that she was just 5 feet 2 inches tall and didn't weigh very much! But, fortunately, the next thing we knew, her voice was no longer shrill, and the client complaints stopped. The whole process of change turned out to be a lot of fun for her, too.

If recording your voice reveals a naturally high or low pitch, work on varying it, and notice what a difference it can make. With just a little bit of practice, you'll find others listening to you more intently.

If pitch turns out to be a big problem for you and trying to change your voice on your own proves too difficult, you might consider working with a vocal coach. It will do your leadership personal brand a lot of good, and it will help you feel more self-confident.

Enunciation. Another aspect of your Sound to focus on is how clearly you articulate words. Speaking succinctly and correctly is important, no matter what personal brand you want to communicate. If you find it difficult to say words clearly, or if you sometimes struggle to pronounce words correctly, here are three steps to consider: Practice, practice, practice.

One way to do this is to audio-record yourself reading articles. Then, play back the recording, and listen to how well you enunciate and pronounce your words. Ask others to listen to your recordings, too, to make sure they can understand everything you say. That will tell you immediately if you're enunciating well enough.

Are you a mutterer? One way to tell is to think back on how often people ask you to repeat what you've just said. If people ask you fairly often—two to three times a day or so—there's a good chance you're mumbling. If you don't pronounce your words clearly, you run the risk of creating a leadership personal brand image that is careless and sloppy—someone who doesn't care about being understood. Or worse, you could come across as someone who isn't very capable, and that's a definite Leadership Personal Brand Buster!

Volume. Avoid speaking too loudly or too softly. No one likes to be shouted at, so if you speak too loudly, you risk communicating a "bully" or domineering leadership personal Brand Character. This is especially true over the phone. Have you ever spoken to someone whose voice was so loud that you had to hold the receiver away from your ear? It can be uncomfortable and annoying, and that isn't the brand you want to communicate.

On the other hand, speaking too softly is simply pointless. This may sound a bit harsh, but honestly, either speak up ... or shut up. It's tiring to have to constantly strain to hear what someone is saying, so it doesn't take long before people will simply stop listening altogether.

Unfortunately, women are often the guiltiest when it comes to low-volume speaking. I once sat on the board of a company whose CFO was a very capable woman. However, in board meetings, she spoke so softly while presenting her financial reports that the entire board would literally lean forward in attempts to hear her. The CEO tried coaching her to speak more loudly, but nothing seemed to work. Out of sheer frustration, she was finally asked to wear a clip microphone on her lapel which she turned on when she wanted to speak. I got the impression that she thought the situation was a bit funny and almost endearing. But it wasn't. All it communicated was poor self-leadership and a weak leadership personal brand. In fact, it made some board members question her ability as a CFO because she just couldn't get past her naturally quiet voice.

If speaking too softly is your challenge, here's something to try: Pretend that the person you are speaking to is located far away in a corner of the room. If you still have trouble projecting, take a few voice lessons.

Talking too much. If you tend to talk a lot, not letting anybody else get a word in edgewise, it's important that you learn to stop, breathe, and *listen.* It's easy to forget to do this when you get excited or nervous, but if you don't, your Audience will eventually tune you out. In fact, people who talk too much can come across as self-centered and unwilling to listen to others, especially if they tend to interrupt. It's not a leadership personal brand "booster," that's for sure.

Not talking enough. The opposite is a problem, too. Are you quiet most of the time? As hard as it may be at first, for the sake of your leadership personal brand, it's critically important to speak up and participate in conversations, especially in meetings. You were invited for a reason—to contribute—so make sure you do.

The power of emotion. Think about dynamic speakers you've listened to. It's the emotions they are able to elicit that have listeners on the edge of their seats. Sure, the words they use may have an impact on you, but if those same words were spoken without much color, they would fall flat. A great leadership personal brand builder knows that just the right amount of emotion to make a point will get the Audience engaged and listening intently to the message.

So, re-listen to your voice recordings, be honest with yourself, and ask: What emotions am I broadcasting through my vocal patterns? Do I sound full of energy and enthusiasm, or do I sound as if I lack commitment? Am I convincing when I speak? If you find you have a monotone voice—the kind that sounds humdrum after a while—practice changing the tone, and work at letting the right kinds of emotions come through your Sound. Again, if this is a particular problem for you and you have the opportunity to work with a vocal coach, it can have a positive impact on your brand. If you're not sure how your emotions carry through your voice, ask others for their opinions.

Telephone. All of the aspects of your Sound that we've talked about so far are just as important to your phone voice as to your in-person voice. Don't underestimate the importance of your Sound in communicating your leadership personal brand by phone. And this applies no matter who you're talking with—a key client, your boss, someone from a different division, a member of your team, a receptionist, etc.

Practicing good phone etiquette with *anyone* is a great leadership personal brand booster. Courtesy, clarity of tone, and articulating words are important. Here are some great tips to communicate YOU™ by phone:

- Practice what you're going to say beforehand, especially if you think you'll need to leave a voicemail message. It helps you to clarify what you want to say, and it can prevent you from stumbling over your words.

- Speak clearly but not too quickly. If you leave your name, slow down, and spell it out. Then, repeat your telephone number to make sure it's understandable.

- Simple courtesies like always thanking the person on the other end of the line and saying goodbye before hanging up go a long way toward establishing who YOU™ are.

Mobile phone. This is one of those things that is easily forgotten, but your mobile phone is also part of your Sound. So, be sure to turn off your phone when you're in meetings, or you risk coming across as rude.

Pay attention to your ring tone, too. Here's a funny mobile phone experience that I had a while back: I was meeting with a potential executive coaching client who held a very senior position in his company. During our meeting—as I sat across from him at his big mahogany desk inside his large and beautifully decorated office, with his two personal assistants sitting outside—this executive's mobile phone rang. I expected a standard ring tone, appropriate for a high-level corporate executive. But that's not what I heard. All of a sudden, out of his phone erupted a wildly raucous hip-hop song playing at full volume! His ring tone wasn't at all what I would have expected for someone of his stature, and I admit: In a single instant, my impression of this man's leadership personal brand changed drastically.

As it turns out, his teenage son had played a practical joke on him and changed his ring tone. Once the executive turned off the phone and shared that fact with me, we both had a good laugh. He even admitted that he just didn't have the technical savvy to figure out how to change the ring tone back, so all he could do was continually apologize for it!

While it was a genuinely funny experience that still makes me chuckle when I think about it, it made me realize that even the ring tones you choose for your mobile phone can impact how others perceive, think, and feel about YOU™.

E-mail: Your "Written Sound"

Even though work e-mails and text messages are written, they still reflect your "Sound." It's a fascinating truth of modern-day communications: We tend to pay close attention to what we write in a formal snail-mail letter, but we can be very careless when it comes to writing e-mails and texts. I've seen people agonize over what will be printed on letterhead, but those same folks will send out rapid-fire e-mails or type quickly on their phones without paying much attention to content or errors. It's critical to remember that your leadership personal brand comes through in these work-related messages just as much as it does in a phone conversation or in person. And just as with speech, communicating your Sound via e-mail and text is often less about *what* you write than it is about *how* you write it.

For example, do you start with a nice greeting, or do you just write a one-line response to the previous question with no sign-off? If you were going to call the colleague you are writing, you wouldn't just state your one-line response and then hang up without a hello or goodbye, would you? It's interesting, but for some reason, we seem to communicate differently via e-mail and text. If they land on the wrong "ears," those short, to-the-point one-liners run the risk of coming across as flippant or rude.

Keep in mind the leadership personal brand you are trying to communicate, and think about how you can use electronic messages to support that. For example, take an extra five seconds to start and end all work-related e-mails and text streams with a simple greeting, as well as a nice closing. It's an opportunity to build a stronger connection with your Audience. And, by doing so, you'll certainly stand out from others who take less care with their messages.

Here are some other things to watch out for when you e-mail and text:

- In your e-mails, include a signature that has your name and telephone number in it. This reminds the recipient of who you are and makes it easy for him or her to contact you. Never require someone—especially a customer—to search through all of your e-mails for the one that includes your phone number.

- Be sure to use spell-check before sending e-mails. With today's technology, spelling errors really shouldn't happen. All that said, you can't always rely on spell-check because it may not pick up every mistake. So, be sure to proofread carefully before hitting the "send" button.

- Make sure your work e-mail subject lines are clear and to the point. Think of subject heads as the title of a document. They should reflect exactly what your e-mail is about.

- A little humor here and there is great to include in e-mails and text messages if you can and if it's consistent with your leadership personal brand, but be careful with jokes at work. It can sometimes be hard to get the real intention across in written form, and you run the risk of being misunderstood.

- Emoticons can be fun in personal communications, but it's best to shy away from using them in a professional message unless you have a strong personal friendship with the person on the receiving end.

Your "Sound" Marketing Plan

It's time to explore the Sound portion of your Leadership Personal Brand Marketing Plan. Let's tune in to our two colleagues to see how each of them will use Sound to communicate their brands.

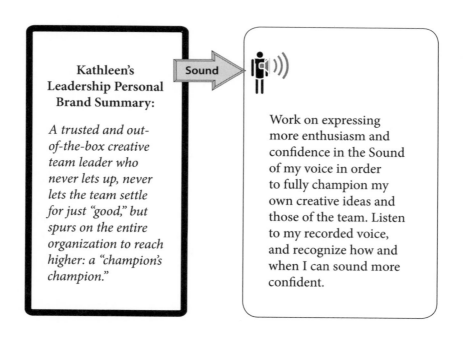

Kathleen's Leadership Personal Brand Summary:

A trusted and out-of-the-box creative team leader who never lets up, never lets the team settle for just "good," but spurs on the entire organization to reach higher: a "champion's champion."

Sound

Work on expressing more enthusiasm and confidence in the Sound of my voice in order to fully champion my own creative ideas and those of the team. Listen to my recorded voice, and recognize how and when I can sound more confident.

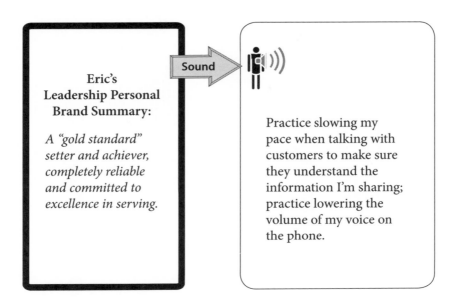

Okay, you know the drill—it's your turn. What is your Sound Marketing Plan? What steps will you take to make sure your Sound reflects your brand as you've defined it?

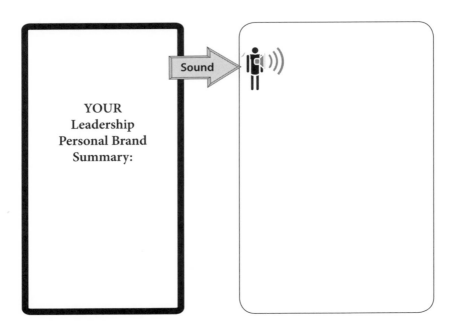

Communicate it

16

Leadership Personal Brand Marketing Plan Activity #5: *Thoughts*

Whether you think you can or whether you think you can't, you're right.

— Henry Ford, founder of the Ford Motor Company

I believe I've saved the best for last when it comes to the five activities that communicate your leadership personal brand: your Thoughts. Why is that? Because your Thoughts are the one activity that can impact every other activity in your Leadership Personal Brand Marketing Plan—your Actions, your Reactions, your Look, and your Sound.

What I'm about to write may sound a bit crazy to you, but bear with me a minute. In the 1600s, Galileo—who is today considered the "Father of Modern Science"—was interrogated for 18 days straight, tortured, imprisoned, and called a heretic. He was then placed under house arrest by the Inquisition for the rest of his life until he died, blind, at the age of 78. He was even buried without a proper monument. What horrible crime had Galileo committed that brought on this brutal treatment?

He wrote and gave lectures supporting the belief that the earth revolves around the sun.

Hard to believe, isn't it? Today, we know it's a fact that the earth revolves around the sun. Indeed, we couldn't imagine it any other way. But in Galileo's time, that idea was considered outrageous.

I tell you Galileo's story in hopes that you'll open your mind as you read this chapter and consider these next words as *possible*, even if they challenge your current belief system. Scientists firmly believe that, in the future, the following three words will be as common and as accepted an idea as our sun-centered solar system is today.

Thoughts are things.

It's true: Science is beginning to prove that Thoughts exist in this world in a very real way—that Thoughts are made up of energy, just like a flower, an animal, or the human body. Even though our Thoughts may not be "seen" like a shoe or "touched" like a feather, Thoughts absolutely, positively exist. (You can't see oxygen either, but it's definitely there.) We can prove that the physical brain exists, but the "thinker"— the part of us that actually thinks our Thoughts—is in many ways still a mystery to us.

We'll focus in this chapter on the power that your Thoughts can have on the consistent communication of your leadership personal brand. Just like you can make choices as to which pen you use or what you do with your computer, you have choices as to how you use your Thoughts to build your leadership personal brand.

Of course, the "things" in our lives that we normally see and touch are usually created by someone else—Toshiba made my computer, for example, and Mont Blanc made my pen. But to me, the most exciting thing about our Thoughts is this: *We* create them. Your thoughts are 100% yours—no one else can create them for you. And that's great news because it means that you have ultimate control over them. You and you alone are responsible for both the Thoughts you think as well as the outcomes of those Thoughts— from start to finish.

In fact, if you think about it (every pun intended), you actually have more control over your Thoughts than you do over a lot of what makes up your Look and your Sound. Even though your brain has some involvement in your thinking, your body isn't really involved with *what* you think. So, you can change your Thoughts at will. It may not be obvious how to do this at first, but your Thoughts offer you an enormous opportunity to impact each and every aspect of your Leadership Personal Brand Marketing Plan.

In short, you can take full control of your personal brand through your Thoughts. It's just a matter of knowing how and making the effort.

Thoughts Are Like Chain Smoking

Psychologists believe that each of us thinks about 60,000 Thoughts per day. That's 3,750 Thoughts per waking hour—a lot by anyone's estimation! But have you ever taken the time to do an "inventory" of your Thoughts? Stop and consider that for a moment. What kinds of Thoughts are *you* creating every hour?

Psychologists also estimate that 95% to 98% of those 60,000 Thoughts each day are repeated the next day, and the next day, and the next. That means only 2% to 5% of our Thoughts are ever really different from one 24-hour period to the next. Our Thoughts are like habits. We stick with the same Thought patterns and stay in the same kind of "Thought rut" day in and day out. You'd think we'd get tired of these same Thoughts, but obviously, we don't even notice that we're thinking the same things over and over. We don't really stop to consider what our heads are filled with day after day.

If you're like most people, your mind has probably picked up some bad habits over the years. It's no wonder that we get into patterns in our lives that we can't seem to shake. In fact, did you ever stop to chew on the idea that it might be your Thoughts that are responsible for negative patterns that play out over and over in your life?

Change Your "Thought Habits"

It's nothing but a good old-fashioned cause-and-effect relationship at work here. Your Thoughts are the cause, and your job, your career, your life, your relationships—and your leadership personal brand—are the effect. If you want to change the "effect"—the outcome—then you need to change the "cause"—your Thoughts. It's really that simple.

Maybe you are saying to yourself, "That sounds good, but how do I actually *do* that?" Just like the bad habits of a chain smoker or someone who drinks too much, it's up to you to change your thinking habits. It takes commitment and focus, but remember that you—and only you—have the power to control what you think about at any point in time. If you don't take charge of what you think, you'll just continue the same old habits that could have a negative impact on your leadership personal brand and, in turn, on your career. It's a powerful element of self-leadership!

There are three key steps to taking charge of your Thoughts:

1. Become aware of your Thoughts.

2. Turn negative Thoughts into positive Thoughts.

3. Embrace positive thinking as a new habit.

Become Aware of Your Thoughts

To change your Thoughts, the first step is to begin paying attention to *what* you think. Of those 3,750 Thoughts running through your head every hour, you're probably not all that conscious of many of them. What's rattling around in your brain all day?

Here's an exercise to help you become more aware of what you are thinking about:

1. Gather two highlighters of different colors, a few pieces of lined paper, and a writing pen. (I have found that this exercise really needs to be done on paper, so please resist the urge to use the computer for it.)

2. Set a timer for five minutes. Then, put your pen to paper, and start writing everything that comes to your mind. Write down every single Thought that pops into your head for those five minutes, and don't let your pen stop. Don't worry about what you've written or whether it makes sense—no one has to read it but you.

3. Once the five minutes is up, read the Thoughts you've written. Take the two colored highlighters, and highlight every thought related to "work" in one color and every thought related to "personal life" in a different color.

4. Then, go back and reread your Thoughts again. This time, with a pen, underline all *negative* Thoughts, and circle all *positive* Thoughts.

5. Now, sit back and look at the outcome:

   • First, which color do you see the most on your pages—the color you chose for work Thoughts, or the color you chose for personal life Thoughts? This tells you what types of Thoughts most prevail in your mind.

- Likewise, are there more underlines (negative Thoughts) or more circles (positive Thoughts) on your pages?

- Dive deeper and investigate:

  - Are your negative Thoughts more related to work or your personal life?

  - What do you think about in positive, not negative, ways?

- What have you learned about your Thoughts from this exercise?

This is a great way to become more aware of the 60,000 Thoughts that you have in a day, and that kind of awareness is the first key step toward changing your Thoughts. If you've discovered that you have a lot of negative Thoughts, don't let your worry about it create yet another negative Thought! Just keep reading, and you'll discover many ways to make sure the way you think doesn't prevent you from getting the leadership personal branding results you want.

Turn Negative Thoughts into Positive Thoughts

Once you are aware of the content of your Thoughts, the second step to managing them effectively is to train yourself to turn negative Thoughts into positive ones. Maybe that sounds hard to do, but there are people all across the globe who manage to keep their Thoughts positive rather than negative.

In fact, do you know people who are just naturally happy—people whose lives seem to always come together for them and fall into place? They have the perfect family, the perfect job, the perfect life. You know the kind of people I'm talking about, right? Well, I believe there's one thing that unites them all: They regularly think positive Thoughts. These people see the glass as half full instead of half empty, guaranteed.

The positive results you see in their lives and in their leadership personal brands are internally driven. People like that just naturally think about how things will turn out *well*, and their Thoughts become a reality. They don't focus on drama or problems. They focus on what the positive outcome will be, and you can see the results of their Thoughts in their lives every single day. What they think actually becomes real.

How are *your* Thoughts impacting your life and your career? Are you one of those people who wake up in the morning and say,

"Ugh! Another day. I have to go to the office and face that pushy office manager again. I just know it's going to be a rotten day." And, of course, because that Thought plays over and over in your mind for the next 24 hours, it's a self-fulfilling prophecy. You proved yourself right, but what did you gain from it?

Instead, what if you practiced powerful self-leadership and changed that initial Thought into something positive? What if the first thing you said to yourself when you woke up was, "Whoo hoo—another day! I look forward to getting to the office and working on building a better relationship with the office manager. That would be a great step toward creating the brand I want for myself and to having a more fulfilling career. It's going to be a productive day!" Think about it: If you could start your mornings with those Thoughts, how different would your days be?

And here's the really exciting thing: Even if you make a positive statement *before you fully believe it*, you will eventually begin to believe it. If you just allow for that small opening of possibility that you *could* have a better day, the door will soon swing wide open for you if you consistently think positively about it.

I'm not advocating that you walk around with the attitude of an over-the-top game show host, but expecting the worst will definitely deliver just that. A powerful coaching technique that addresses this is coined as turning "ANTS into PETS"—shifting "**A**utomatic **N**egative **T**houghts" into "**P**erformance-**E**nhancing **T**houghts." Which do you have more of—ANTS or PETS?

Homework Assignment

Every morning this week when you wake up, condition yourself to let the very first thing that pops into your head be a positive thought. I guarantee that, after doing this regularly for a while, you'll be amazed what a difference it makes in the outlook of your day.

Does thinking more positively sound challenging to you? The truth is that managing your Thoughts is far from rocket science or magic. It's actually incredibly simple, and—as we said earlier—*you* are in charge.

For example:

- Do you want your Audience to perceive, think, and feel that your leadership personal brand is "creative"? Then, think creative Thoughts.

- Do you want your Audience to treat you nicely? Then, think nice thoughts about your Audience.

- Do you want to feel more at peace at work? Then, think more peaceful thoughts about work.

Embrace Positive Thinking as a New Habit

We've covered steps 1 and 2: Become aware of your Thoughts, and turn negative Thoughts into positive ones. Now, let's move on to our third step toward taking charge of your Thoughts—embracing positive thinking as a new self-leadership habit.

Earlier in my life, I struggled with this as well. Then, I stumbled upon a Buddhist monk in Thailand who helped me a great deal to change my Thought habits. He said that our minds can be like an untamed monkey, always jumping about actively, running here and there. To train it, you have to learn to reel in the monkey, as though it were on a chain, until it is fully within your control. You can choose when to reel in your "monkey mind" and when to let it run wild again. It's your mind, after all! Let's put it this way: Either you control your mind and your Thoughts, or your mind and your Thoughts control you. I know which one I prefer. How about you?

Grabbing Your Monkey Mind by the Tail

There are a lot of ways you can take control of your Thoughts. Reel in that monkey mind, grab it by the tail, and make it your pet—not the other way around. Then and only then can positive thinking become your way of being. Here are some tips for reeling in your monkey mind:

1. **Take charge!** Tell your mind that *you* are the one in control here and that you simply won't allow any negative Thoughts to interfere with building the leadership personal brand that you want and deserve.

2. **Switch from negative to positive.** If you find that your Thoughts are running amuck with fear, wondering, questioning, and "what if" scenarios, start training yourself to switch your thinking to something positive. Create a list of the happiest moments in your life, making sure to write them in detail. For example, don't just write: "The day I was promoted to Senior Operations Manager." Instead, create a list that will really help you when you're feeling down by reminding you exactly how you felt during that proud moment. Write something like: "The day when I was promoted to Senior Operations Manager, my boss called me into a conference room and congratulated me in front of the whole team. Everyone applauded, and I felt like I was walking on air. I was so proud and happy that my accomplishments had been recognized. It was clear that my boss and my team really appreciated my efforts on the job and that the company trusted me to take on these important responsibilities."

Then, when you need to switch your thinking from something negative, focus your mind on one of the positive memories on your list. Relive it as best you can. Close your eyes for a moment, and remember any sights, sounds, smells, textures, or tastes to help you mentally return to that time. The more you practice this exercise, the more quickly you will be able to transform your negative Thoughts into positive ones. In fact, eventually, all you will have to do is think, "my salesperson of the month award," for example, and you'll automatically be able to shift your focus and get rid of those negative Thoughts.

3. **Remember that Thoughts are also Reactions, just like physical Reactions.** Are your Thought Reactions out of control? When a difficult event occurs at work, you may control what you say and do, but do your Thoughts go wild? Do you immediately jump to conclusions or become furious at someone else inside of your head? If so, think seriously about how these Thoughts are serving you, especially if you end up shouting at someone in your mind for days on end. Who is that really impacting?

It's easy to become consumed with emotions in your mind, but they rob you of a lot of energy and keep you focused on negative Thoughts. The next time you have a knee-jerk Thought Reaction, catch yourself. Work on letting go of the negative emotion surrounding the situation as quickly as possible. Otherwise, you will let the situation control you, rather than the other way around. Avoid thinking in terms of who's right and who's wrong. If you're wasting your time on negative Thoughts just because you believe you'll win an argument, you've already lost! Remember that just as you have the power to control your physical Reactions, you can also control your Thought Reactions.

Whenever coaching clients are having negative thoughts, I suggest they move into an unemotional, objective space—as though they were "outside" of themselves. From this "observer" place, they can assess the Thought without any attachment to it. The observer might think, "That's an interesting Thought, but it isn't serving me very well right now. I'm going to consciously replace it with a positive Thought." Many clients tell me that this technique helps them shift from negativity to positivity more easily than any other.

4. **Set goals for changing your Thought patterns**. Your goals should be achievable, but realistic and measurable in some way. By doing so, you'll know exactly when you've achieved success. For example: "Between now and 3:00 p.m., every time I catch myself thinking a non-leadership-personal-brand-building Thought, I'm going to switch my thinking to _____ instead." It takes focus and effort, but hopefully, you can see how this trains your monkey mind and reels it in over time.

5. **Reward yourself for reaching your goals and thinking positive brand-building Thoughts.** Take an inventory at the end of each day. If the majority of your Thoughts were positive, treat yourself to a visit to Starbucks on the way home, or take yourself to a movie. Once your mind catches on that you're going to be rewarded for thinking positive Thoughts, it will be much easier to tame. Eventually, thinking positively will simply become a natural way of life for you.

6. **Affirm what you want.** You have probably heard about positive affirmations, and maybe you've even used them in the past. They really are a powerful way to alter your Thoughts. Think of all of the positive affirmations you can say about yourself around work.

For example:

- "I do a great job of communicating my leadership personal brand."

- "I come across as charismatic to my Audience, and they see me as confident and professional."

- "My work is appreciated and recognized by my boss, colleagues, and clients."

It's important that every affirmation be written or spoken in present tense, as if it's already truth. That's the point! You don't have to fully believe the affirmation for it to begin to impact the way you think, but the key is to strive to believe these affirmations more and more as you regularly say, read, and/or write them.

Make affirmations a regular part of your day. Read them first thing in the morning, at lunch time, and right before you go to sleep. If you can, read them out loud, and really "feel" what it's like to have that affirmation be real. Envision yourself as you will be once these statements are reality. Some people even write each affirmation in a notebook 20 or more times per day. Do what it takes to get your mind wrapped around the image of the powerful leadership personal brand you want.

By following these tips, I'm not saying that nothing painful will ever happen to you again. But your attitude about what does happen to you will become positive enough that you can get through difficult situations easier.

A strong, positive mental attitude will create more miracles than any wonder drug.

— Patricia Neal, actress

The "Picture" of Success

Top actors and athletes often say that they *envision* their success. They actually picture themselves getting the job, giving a great performance, winning the game, or crossing the finish line first. Many of them swear by this method for not only staying positively focused before a big event, but for turning what they envision into reality.

Let's apply this to YOU™. Try playing out "tomorrows" in your mind. How are people responding to you? How are you responding to them? How do you present yourself? How do you look? How does it feel when everyone recognizes what YOU™ have to offer? What does it feel like to be charismatic? Picture yourself successfully putting your Leadership Personal Brand Marketing Plan into effect.

The key is to turn your Thoughts into activities, and make your vision real. It *is* in your control, and the more you are truly able to sense this as reality in your mind, the closer you will be to making it reality in your life and in your career.

However You Slice It: Negative Thoughts are Negative Things

Still not convinced that Thoughts are things? Whether or not you can completely buy into the science of Thought, no matter how you look at it, life is frankly just a lot more satisfying when you stay positive and in control of what you think. And it's hard to argue with the fact that people with negative attitudes are simply a lot less enjoyable to have as friends, employees, or business partners. There isn't any benefit in communicating a negative leadership personal brand. No matter how much work you put into the other aspects of your brand, negative Thoughts will prevent you from fully making YOU™ a reality. Your Audience won't perceive, think, and feel in a positive way about your leadership personal brand as long as negative Thoughts are in the way.

As the world becomes more aware of the power of our minds, more books and films like *The Law of Attraction* and *The Secret* will enter the mainstream. Today, it's becoming more accepted to believe that our lives are really just reflections of our attitudes and Thoughts. We're beginning to see that simple changes within our minds can create real change in our lives and, collectively, in the world.

Your "Thoughts" Marketing Plan

So, how will you work on your Thoughts in your Leadership Personal Brand Marketing Plan? Let's see what our two colleagues are going to do to take charge of their Thoughts.

Kathleen's Leadership Personal Brand Summary:

A trusted and out-of-the-box creative team leader who never lets up, never lets the team settle for just "good," but spurs on the entire organization to reach higher: a "champion's champion."

Thoughts

Pay closer attention to insecure Thoughts about my creative abilities. Make a list of positive Thoughts to replace those negative Thoughts.

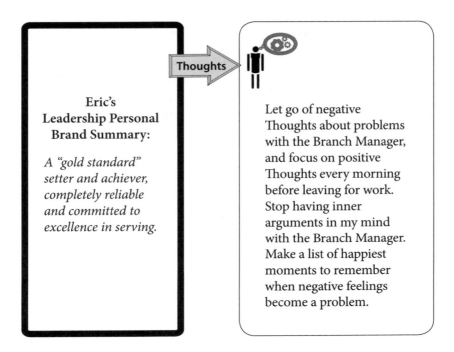

Eric's Leadership Personal Brand Summary:

A "gold standard" setter and achiever, completely reliable and committed to excellence in serving.

Let go of negative Thoughts about problems with the Branch Manager, and focus on positive Thoughts every morning before leaving for work. Stop having inner arguments in my mind with the Branch Manager. Make a list of happiest moments to remember when negative feelings become a problem.

You're now ready to pull together your entire Leadership Personal Brand Marketing Plan. This is the heart and soul of making your desired personal brand a reality.

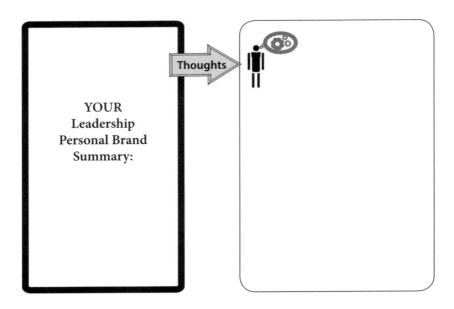

YOUR Leadership Personal Brand Summary:

Communicate it

Leadership
Personal Brand Marketing Plan

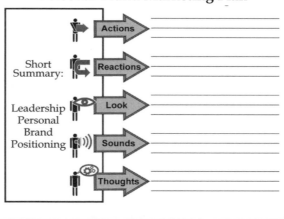

Short
Summary:

Leadership
Personal
Brand
Positioning

Actions

Reactions

Look

Sounds

Thoughts

17

Your Complete Leadership Personal Brand Marketing Plan

Good plans make good decisions. That's why good planning helps make elusive dreams come true.

— Lester Robert Bittel, author

You have carefully defined your brand using the six elements that make up YOU™. You've looked in-depth at all five activities that communicate your leadership personal brand and that make up your Leadership Personal Brand Marketing Plan. Now, it's time to combine all of the activities together, so I encourage you to capture all five activities on one page.

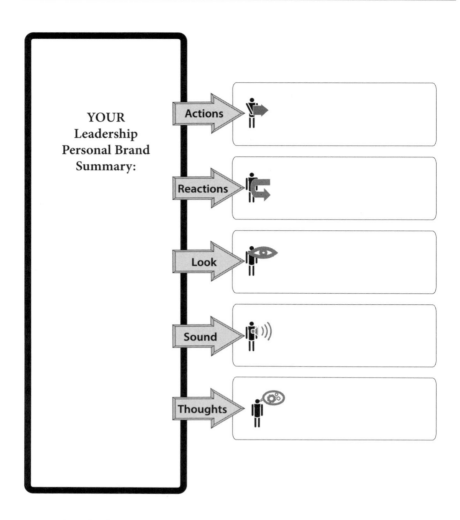

Take a look at the completed Marketing Plans for Kathleen and Eric on the pages that follow. This is how they plan to work on their Actions, Reactions, Look, Sound, and Thoughts to create greater success in their careers. As you look at their Marketing Plans, hopefully, you can see a full picture of how both Kathleen and Eric are taking charge of their leadership personal brands.

As you review their plans, think about how you might want to make adjustments to your own. Once you see all five of your Marketing Plan activities together, does anything else come to mind that would strengthen each activity and propel you closer toward YOU™?

Kathleen's Leadership Personal Brand Marketing Plan

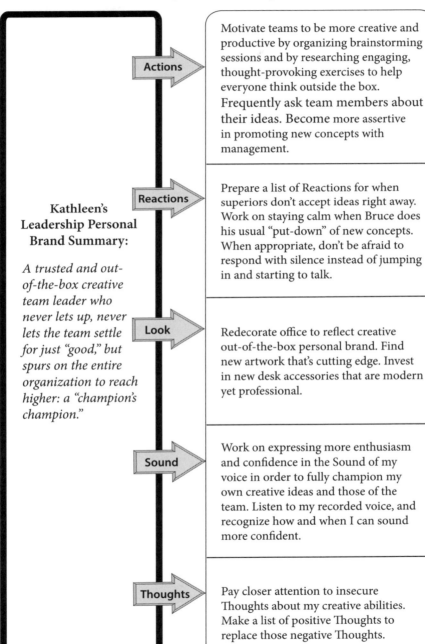

Actions

Motivate teams to be more creative and productive by organizing brainstorming sessions and by researching engaging, thought-provoking exercises to help everyone think outside the box. Frequently ask team members about their ideas. Become more assertive in promoting new concepts with management.

Reactions

Prepare a list of Reactions for when superiors don't accept ideas right away. Work on staying calm when Bruce does his usual "put-down" of new concepts. When appropriate, don't be afraid to respond with silence instead of jumping in and starting to talk.

Look

Redecorate office to reflect creative out-of-the-box personal brand. Find new artwork that's cutting edge. Invest in new desk accessories that are modern yet professional.

Sound

Work on expressing more enthusiasm and confidence in the Sound of my voice in order to fully champion my own creative ideas and those of the team. Listen to my recorded voice, and recognize how and when I can sound more confident.

Thoughts

Pay closer attention to insecure Thoughts about my creative abilities. Make a list of positive Thoughts to replace those negative Thoughts.

Kathleen's Leadership Personal Brand Summary:

A trusted and out-of-the-box creative team leader who never lets up, never lets the team settle for just "good," but spurs on the entire organization to reach higher: a "champion's champion."

Eric's Leadership Personal Brand Marketing Plan

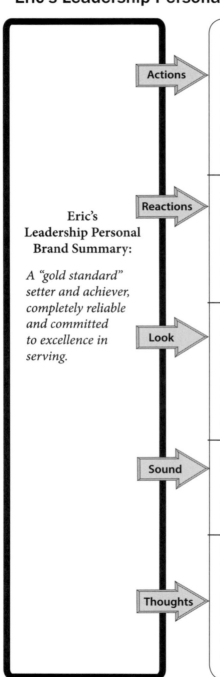

Eric's Leadership Personal Brand Summary:

A "gold standard" setter and achiever, completely reliable and committed to excellence in serving.

Actions

Volunteer for Personal Banker tasks, such as researching the accounts of key clients and determining what other products and services might be helpful to them. Take a leadership role in Branch Manager training programs, and create lesson plans and case studies for trainees based on my specific experiences with clients.

Reactions

Practice positive self-talk in difficult situations with the Branch Manager, reminding myself not to take her stress personally; prepare and anticipate various applicable Reactions for frustrated customers in order to keep my cool.

Look

Take better care of my skin and hands—they're in front of customers all the time. Keep nails in shape by having a basic manicure the last Thursday evening of every month. Invest in odorless hand lotion to keep hands from getting so rough due to working with documents and papers all day long.

Sound

Practice slowing my pace when talking with customers to make sure they understand the information I'm sharing; practice lowering the volume of my voice on the phone.

Thoughts

Let go of negative Thoughts about problems with the Branch Manager, and focus on positive Thoughts every morning before leaving for work. Stop having inner arguments in my mind with the Branch Manager. Make a list of happiest moments to remember when negative feelings become a problem.

YOUR Leadership Personal Brand Marketing Plan

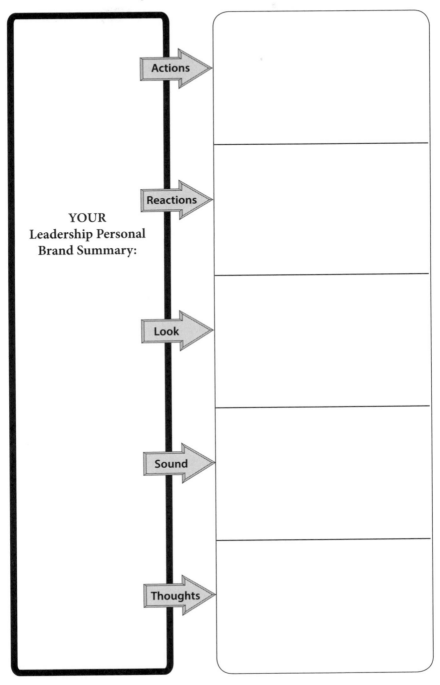

Find Meaning in the Menial

Now that your Marketing Plan is mapped out, it's important to keep it handy. Laminate it, post it on your desk, put it on your iPad, make it your wallpaper on your smartphone, tape it inside your desk drawer, or use it as your computer screen saver. Just make sure that you have it in front of you regularly to remind you of the steps that YOU™ need to take to achieve your desired leadership personal brand.

Keeping this in mind will allow you to do what I call "find meaning in the menial." This means that even the little mundane tasks you do every day at work can now stand for something. Each and every task is yet one more chance to communicate what you want your leadership personal brand to be.

Do you want to communicate "team player" as part of your leadership personal brand? Try pitching in to help tidy up the office kitchen or make an extra pot of coffee. Again, these are fairly menial tasks, but they represent additional opportunities to communicate YOU™.

Does your leadership personal brand have a lot to do with being reliable? Make sure you're always at your desk a few minutes early in the morning and that you're back from lunch right on time. Finish your most important tasks before you leave.

Hopefully, you can now begin to see how any work task, no matter how boring, can still be part of building your leadership personal brand. Don't underestimate the power of the "little things" in communicating a great deal about who you are and what YOU™ stand for. You never know how something seemingly small may actually be "large" in the eyes of your Audience.

Here's an example: Phyllis was a Computer Networking Project Manager whose Desired Identity was to be "the networking project manager from heaven." She began to accomplish her goal in small ways, but she had no idea the impact some of her tiny efforts would have. That is, until a customer named Brett called one day with a problem. Phyllis not only did her job and did it well, solving Brett's problem as quickly as possible, but she also offered Brett an extra quick tip to help him utilize his network more efficiently. The next day, Phyllis was called in to her director's office and told that Brett had called the company to compliment Phyllis for her excellent work. The tip Phyllis had given Brett proved to be enormously helpful. What Phyllis didn't know was that Brett was actually the son of a major shareholder of the company. Not long afterward,

Phyllis received a nice, unexpected cash bonus as a reward for her extra effort.

Never lose track of the fact that you're building a relationship with your Audience with every interaction, and that even those who are *not* on your immediate Audience list may still talk to your Audience about you. In any meeting, whether in a conference room, on the elevator, at a podium, via phone, via Skype, via e-mail, via text, or on social media, take the opportunity to communicate your leadership personal brand. You never know what might come of seemingly unimportant exchanges. Make every moment count, and be consistent day in and day out.

We've made it through Steps 1 and 2 of the *Master the Brand Called YOU™* personal branding system, helping you define your leadership personal brand and determining how to communicate it every day via your Marketing Plan. There's just one more step to go: to make sure that you don't *damage* this leadership personal brand called YOU™ that you've worked so hard to develop.

Step 3
Avoid Damaging it

Leadership Personal Brand Busters®

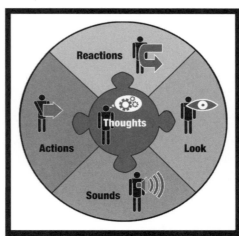

18

Leadership Personal Brand Busters®

Learn from the mistakes of others—you can never live long enough to make them all yourself.

> — John Luther Long, author of the short story "Madame Butterfly"

E ven though the above quote makes me chuckle, I actually take these words to heart. That's why over the years, I've developed a long list of what I call "Leadership Personal Brand Busters."

What are those? Well, simply put, Leadership Personal Brand Busters are Actions, Reactions, Looks, Sounds, or Thoughts that are inconsistent with, or contrary to, your leadership personal brand. They're what you *don't* want to do while trying to communicate a powerful leadership personal brand. Left uncaught, these Busters can work against all of the effort you've made so far to build your brand. Leadership Personal Brand Busters can slow down your progress toward a desired job promotion, prevent you from getting raises, and even cause you to derail your career.

For more than two decades, I've collected and developed a long list of Busters through working in and with large corporations around the world. I've also collected many as a result of starting up and running my own business, and through coaching others toward defining and communicating their own unique leadership personal brands. Of course, some Leadership Personal Brand Busters are mistakes that I've made myself in the process of developing my own leadership personal brand, and I'm happy to share them with you in hopes of sparing you the embarrassments I've occasionally suffered!

The intention behind these Busters is—as John Luther Long said —to help you learn from the mistakes of people like me and the people I've observed, so that you can avoid committing these Busters and damaging your own leadership personal brand. As Benjamin Franklin once said, "It takes many good deeds to build a good reputation and only one bad one to lose it."

Let's be honest: Every one of us is guilty of a few Leadership Personal Brand Busters from time to time, and we often don't even realize we're committing them. That's why I want to share with you the following 20 Busters (four for each of our five Leadership Personal Brand Marketing Plan activities) so that you can keep an especially watchful eye out for these Busters as you put your Marketing Plan into action. These 20 Leadership Personal Brand Busters are some of the most common ones that I've witnessed over the years related to self-leadership.

Keep in mind that this list is not the "final" list of Leadership Personal Brand Busters by any means. In fact, there is no end to the potential list of Busters that might rear their ugly heads! You will definitely come up with other Busters that are unique to your job or to your situation. In fact, you should. When you do, write them down, and start your own list.

It's important to remember that Leadership Personal Brand Busters are self-leadership behaviors you might be doing either consciously or unconsciously. So, you have to keep a watchful eye out for them, as they may be like stealth bombers—often under your conscious radar.

How do you know when you've come across a Leadership Personal Brand Buster?

1. Recognize when you've made an error in judgment, and make note of it in order to avoid repeating the mistake. There's the beginning of your own Leadership Personal Brand Busters list.

2. Watch others, and observe what they do or say that hurts their images. You'll learn a lot about how to avoid damaging your own leadership personal brand in the process.

The Leadership Personal Brand Busters in the next chapter apply to anyone who wants to come across as professional, confident, reliable, and in control—self-leadership characteristics that most of us aspire to communicate with our brands at work. Take a moment to read through each one, think about it, and be honest with yourself. Have you fallen prey to any of these Busters? If you aren't sure, ask someone close to you to give you an objective and honest perspective. Only then can you be sure that your leadership personal brand is being communicated as you want and that it is working to bring YOU™ the kind of success you deserve.

"Just remember, success is built upon avoiding
Personal Brand Busters®"

19

Quiz: Common Leadership Personal Brand Busters®

I never make stupid mistakes. Only very, very clever ones.
— John Peel, British broadcaster

Mistakes aren't stupid unless we don't learn from them. In fact, I side with Peel: Most mistakes are actually "very, very clever" because they open doors to help us get better at communicating our leadership personal brands.

As I said in the previous chapter, that's what Leadership Personal Brand Busters are all about—learning from the mistakes that others have made along the way toward building their brands. You can hopefully avoid damaging your own brand by keeping those mistakes top of mind. They are the pitfalls and traps to watch out for as you begin to put your Leadership Personal Brand Marketing Plan into action.

On the following pages, you will find 20 of the most common Leadership Personal Brand Busters I've run across. They are divided up into four Busters each of the five Marketing Plan Activities: Actions, Reactions, Look, Sound, and Thoughts.

After you have finished reading them, take the quiz at the end of this chapter, and test yourself on how often you commit these Leadership Personal Brand Busters.You will then know exactly how much work you need to do to bust these common Busters.

Leadership Personal Brand Busters—Actions

1. **Offering an inappropriate handshake.** Is your handshake too weak? I've had the most amazingly burly men offer me handshakes that were so "wimpy" that they completely destroyed my impression of their initial leadership personal brand image. No matter how you look, if you don't offer a handshake that comes across as confident, you'll undermine your leadership personal brand. In the global work world, the handshake is still the most common means of greeting each other. Often, before you exchange business cards or even open your mouth, you're shaking someone's hand and making a first impression with your grip.

   On the other hand, is your handshake just the *opposite* of wimpy? I've had some people crush my hand so badly with a forceful handshake that my ring engraved itself into my finger in a matter of seconds. What kind of leadership personal brand message do you think that person is communicating? A bully? Someone who must have their way by force? Either way, it doesn't communicate the kind of person I would want to work with.

   I don't know of any school that offers a course in "Handshake 101," so unfortunately, most of us are not taught the best way to shake hands. Practice your handshake if you aren't sure about it. It should be firm and link thumb-to-thumb with the other person. If you're afraid of being too forceful or not sure if you're squeezing too hard, ask someone you trust to be honest with you. Whatever you do, make sure your handshake is communicating your brand effectively. If not, it will leave behind a leadership personal brand impression that may be hard to ... well, *shake.*

2. **Asking permission to make decisions within your scope of responsibility.** Have you ever noticed how very successful people don't ask for permission? They ask for forgiveness instead. They just make decisions and take action. This is true of strong brand builders as well.

   I'm not encouraging you to take charge and make decisions *outside* of your scope of responsibility. But, *within* that scope, have enough confidence in your own ability to make decisions without asking first. If your scope of responsibility is undefined, or if there are areas where you'd like to have greater responsibility, sit down with your boss and map it out. Say something like, "I want to be able to make decisions in this area without asking for permission. Help me define that. How can I determine where you want me to ask your permission and where you don't?" This is a powerful leadership personal brand builder.

3. **Working on less important, easier tasks before tackling the tough ones.** Successful brand builders define their priorities every morning and stick to them. So should you. Be disciplined—jump in and tackle the most difficult and most important challenges first. If you do all of the easy tasks first, you'll probably be so tired at the end of the day that you won't have the energy to complete the more challenging tasks that may very well be the most important tasks for your career. Successful leadership personal brand builders focus on the toughest tasks first—and the ones that will satisfy their Audience's Needs the most—to ensure that their best efforts go toward performing the most important work.

4. **Working non-stop without taking a break.** This may appear on the surface to be a good thing. You look like you're working hard and giving it your all, right? Well, actually, it most likely sends a signal that you're in a panic about getting your work done. Or that you're not talented enough to get it done well and in an efficient and effective way. Instead, take 15 minutes now and then to go to the water cooler, stretch your legs, or take a walk. It will not only put you in a better state of mind, but if you're like me, some of the best solutions to problems often come when you step away from a task for a few minutes to refuel. Take the time to rejuvenate yourself for the work ahead, *and* send a signal to others that you're in control of your work and of your leadership personal brand.

Leadership Personal Brand Busters—Reactions

1. **Taking yourself and the situation too seriously.** When I was still relatively junior in my marketing career, I was in charge of managing four laundry detergent brands for Procter & Gamble in Poland. We were in the middle of the annual, often-dreaded event called "Budget Season," during which each brand team had

to ask for and justify every penny of the millions of dollars we would spend on marketing our brands in the coming year. Even though it was a great learning experience, it added considerably more work to our regular 10-hour workdays, so Budget Season was, to be honest, a downright exhausting time.

I remember one Tuesday night during such a Budget Season when the final budget meeting was looming—just 2½ days away. It was 8:30 p.m., and my brand teams and I had just left a meeting with our director who had made several changes to our plans—changes that would mean many, many more hours of work. We had already been on the job since 7:00 that morning, and it was clear that we now had at least three to four more hours of work remaining that night. Everyone was exhausted, hungry, and on edge.

As we returned to our various offices, we each heard that familiar "you've-got-mail" sound emanating from our computers. Everyone glanced down and saw an e-mail from the director whose office we had just left. The subject—written in all caps—said "URGENT REMINDER." Our hearts sank as we anticipated more work to do. What else could he possibly ask of us at this point?

With dread, I opened the e-mail to find that the note only contained three simple words—words I will never forget:

It's only soap.

The director was right, of course! It was his gentle reminder that we were taking the situation too seriously. No matter what we did, it *was* just laundry soap. No one was going to lose a limb or end up homeless as a result of a botched Budget Season.

To this day, when I'm getting uptight about a situation, I stop and remind myself, "It's only soap." Are *you* taking yourself or the situation too seriously? Remember: A little bit of laughter and fun can go a long way toward building your leadership personal brand.

2. **Acting like you understand something when you really don't.** Through coaching over 700 executives in my career, I have found that one of the worst fears we have is to look stupid. We're afraid of appearing foolish, so we don't ask questions. But I actually think the truth is: It's stupid *not* to ask questions. There's no upside to not asking, but there is plenty of downside.

Let's say that you've been given a task to complete, but you're not sure of the objectives, and you didn't ask for clarification for fear of looking stupid. So, where does that leave you? You might end up doing nothing at all because you don't know what to do. Or you could end up taking action that isn't correct because you were afraid to ask what was required to do it right. You then simply waste time doing the wrong thing because you lack the information you need, and you'll more than likely end up missing your deadline because you didn't seek clarity. So, there you are—exposed for not understanding the objectives anyway! In the end, *not* asking questions can leave you looking more foolish than if you had asked questions in the first place. What kind of leadership personal brand message does *that* communicate?

Personally, I love working with people who ask for clarification. It lets me know that they want to get it right the first time, and that they won't stop asking until they fully understand it. Now, who in their right mind would consider *that* stupid?

3. **Consistently giving up previously scheduled personal plans for work.** Denise was an advertising executive who loved her work and wanted desperately to move up in her company. She was in the office before her boss arrived in the morning and was there late at night. She even worked during an offsite office get-together to celebrate a colleague's promotion, thinking that this would help her look better in the eyes of the people who could offer *her* a promotion. Her strategy backfired, though, and her boss called her in to a one-on-one meeting, saying that he was worried about her "workaholism." He even asked if she was all right. He wondered if something might be wrong with her marriage, and he encouraged Denise to spend more time with her family. Denise left the meeting embarrassed, having learned a difficult lesson about the role that work/life balance plays in creating a powerful personal brand.

Once in a while, it's okay to put work first and cancel personal plans. After all, it shows that you're devoted to your Audience/your job/your company/your customers and that you're willing to go the extra mile to get the job done. But if you do this too often, it can come across as needy—or worse, that you're not in control. It can look as though you're desperate and have no life outside the office. People like to work with others who are balanced and live a satisfying personal life. And that makes for a much more interesting leadership personal brand, too.

So, don't always say "yes" to working on weekends and/or evenings. Take a polite stand when appropriate, and make it clear that you have prior plans. Of course, also promise that the work will get finished, and find another way to meet your Audience's Need, as possible.

4. **"Delegating back up" when you can't complete an assigned task.** Very early in my career, I had a demanding boss who taught me an important lesson. He asked me to find out how we could automate the tracking of promotion results on a weekly basis. This was during the earlier days of personal computers, so the task was quite a challenge.

   At first, I was excited about the idea of the automation, so I dug right into it. But I kept hitting one roadblock after another (no good software back then!) until I finally came to the conclusion that what my boss wanted simply wasn't possible. I went back into my boss's office and clearly explained to him all of the reasons why the automation couldn't be done.

   When I finished, he sat quietly looking at me for what felt like forever before saying, "I don't think you understood what I asked you to do. I didn't ask you to tell me that it's not possible. I asked you to tell me how it *is* possible. Don't bring me your problems. Bring me solutions. That's what I pay you for."

   Ouch! It was a bit harsh, but he was right. I had basically delegated the problem back up to him. I didn't offer him possible solutions; I just plopped the challenges right back on his desk. Even if I didn't see any obvious solutions, it was my job to at least offer possibilities. As he pointed out, I was being paid to think through challenges and offer suggestions. That's what good leadership personal brand builders do.

   Learn from my lesson, and if you're ever in a similar situation, think of options to explore even if you can't figure out a way to do exactly what was asked of you. You'll be seen as a valuable, innovative person, which is a great leadership personal brand to own.

Leadership Personal Brand Busters—Look

1. **Underestimating the impact of proper eye contact.** In many business contexts, direct eye contact is critical. It says a great deal about your honesty and level of confidence. Watch television interviewers to see how well they vary their eye contact. They are very good at this, and you can learn a lot from observing them.

   Of course, try to avoid the intimidating "stare-down" that can be equally as uncomfortable as averting your gaze. Staring at someone makes you appear as though you're trying to dominate, while looking down may communicate low self-esteem or nervousness.

   Good leadership personal brand builders make sure to adjust their eye contact for the context of the situation. For example, in Asia and certain other parts of the world, looking someone in the eye who is older or who holds a higher position can be perceived as rude and disrespectful. I was once listening to a Thai monk speak as he presided over the blessing of a new factory, and I looked him in the eye. He later told one of my Thai contacts that I was "out of order." So, in today's increasingly global work world, it's important to be aware of any cultural biases related to eye contact.

2. **Dressing inappropriately for the situation.** Making poor clothing choices—either dressing down or over-dressing—can make everyone uncomfortable and undermine your brand. Find out in advance about the right dress code before showing up to a work event.

   Are you hoping for a promotion? If so, look "up" to see how senior, respected leaders are dressing at your company. Then, follow their lead. You'll be dressing like the leadership personal brand you're working to create.

3. **Thinking that "Look" only means aspects of your person or your office.** Your Look doesn't stop with your clothes, your body, your face, or even your office. It extends to every location where you're responsible for *its* Look.

   A personal story from my days at a multinational corporation illustrates this point. I received a call one day from my boss

214 Master the Brand Called YOU™

informing me that a group of senior leaders were heading to the factory for an important meeting, and the Vice President of Operations was going to drive all of us there since he had the largest car. This man was pulling in a healthy six-figure income and had a beautifully adorned, enormous office in the executive wing. He was incredibly smart, and I was in awe of him at the time. As we were all walking to the parking lot, I had visions of us heading toward a luxurious, high-end vehicle that would mirror this VP's gorgeous office, and I was secretly looking forward to seeing it.

Instead, when we arrived at his car, it was all I could do to keep my jaw from dropping! In the backseat—amidst long, white dog hair all over the faded blue interior—were old bottles and trash that covered the floor as well as the seat. There was an open book on the dashboard (was he reading while driving?) and a broken sun visor that hung down in the front passenger's seat. The state of this VP's car caused my image of him to burst like a bubble, and I'll never forget the experience. The leadership brand I perceived, thought, and felt about this leader changed dramatically from that moment on, and I admit I never looked at him quite the same after that. It made me realize how impactful other "extensions of YOU™" can be in sending inconsistent messages about your brand as a leader.

4. **Ignoring the importance of breath and body odor as part of your "Look."** Many years ago, I had a direct report named Dennis, a young man who was in his first job out of university. He really wanted to succeed, and he was extremely bright and capable. He always had good ideas, was full of energy, and was very enthusiastic about the job. He worked long hard days, and I really enjoyed having him as a direct report.

The problem was that Dennis had bad body odor. Exceptionally bad. He smelled so badly on certain days that when he was in a meeting room with others, they found excuses to cut the meeting short. No one could handle the smell.

One day, the situation came to a head when the General Manager of the company called me to come to his office. He said to me, "I won't attend any more meetings with Dennis until his body odor issues are resolved. I can't handle it anymore, and if he can't learn to bathe properly, we really have to consider his future in this company. Figure out how to handle it, Brenda."

You can imagine how much I dreaded the conversation I was going to have to have with Dennis! It was such a sensitive topic, and I didn't want him to be embarrassed or lose confidence. But I also wanted him to succeed at the company, and I felt he had a bright future. So, not long after that, I set up a meeting with Dennis.

I found out that Dennis swam every morning before he came to work and took a shower right after. So, he was actually very clean. But after he swam and showered, he *put on the same clothes, day after day*. This was because he didn't yet have enough money to invest in more business suits. And the suits he did own had to be dry cleaned, which he couldn't afford to have done on a regular basis.

I reminded Dennis that his professional image was built not just on the way he looked but also on other "sensory" perceptions. We agreed that he would seek out a small loan—just enough to buy a total of two to three more suits and several shirts. As a result, the odor problem disappeared immediately, and I was excited to find out not long ago that Dennis continues to do well in his career, progressing to increasingly higher levels within the same company. This story could have ended in a very different way if Dennis hadn't come around to the realization that our "Look" means more than just what we see with the eyes.

Leadership Personal Brand Busters—Sound

1. **Ignoring the importance of silence as a powerful Sound.** You probably know people who feel a constant need to say something, anything. Whenever there's a moment of quiet, they jump in and speak—even if it's to say something unimportant. These folks are uncomfortable with silence. But they really shouldn't be. Take it from the experts: Ever notice how effective public speakers use silence to make their points? A few moments of silence can be extremely powerful.

   Andre Kostelanetz, a 20th century Russian conductor, once said, "One of the greatest sounds of them all—and to me, it is a sound—

is utter, complete silence." Think about it. Without the rests in music, there would be no rhythm. Speech has rhythm, too. So, what is true in music is true in our communications at work. Sometimes, just sitting back and listening (or being quiet while thinking) is the best Sound you can make. It conveys confidence, intelligence, patience, and reflection. Not a bad leadership personal brand to communicate by saying nothing at all!

2. **Feeling the need to fill silence with "ums."** Occasionally, when people are uncomfortable with silence, they say "um" in the spaces. I watched a television show recently about how a particular movie was produced, and the main female celebrity was interviewed. When she is acting, this actress comes across as well-spoken, capable, and in control. But in this interview—speaking as her real self—every fifth word or so was an "um." It really changed my impression of her, from "confident and poised" to "unsure and inarticulate." I was reminded of Sound Leadership Personal Brand Buster #1: She would have been better off not saying anything at all rather than constantly repeating "um."

I think most people say "um" because they are unsure about what they want to communicate and feel that they should say *something* to fill a quiet moment. Or they want to keep the attention of others but aren't sure what to say next. Still, "um" doesn't add anything to the conversation, and—as illustrated by the example of the celebrity—it can actually damage the way people perceive, think, and feel about you.

Are you unsure if you're saying "um" when you speak? Make a recording of yourself when you give a speech or presentation. Count the "ums" that you say, and upon re-listening, pause and think about the reasons *why* you said "um." When do you say "um," and what's going on in your Thoughts during those moments? You may discover patterns that you can stop. You can also have a friend or a colleague count your "ums" while you speak. You could even start an "Um Fund," and discipline yourself to put a coin into a jar every time you say "um." It will help you become more aware of your "ums" so that you can catch yourself before saying them. Confident leadership personal brand builders replace "ums" with calm silence while thinking about what to say next.

3. **Not speaking up at a meeting you've been invited to attend.** The other extreme, of course, is not contributing at all in a meeting where you've been invited to participate. While you don't want to be a motor-mouth or say "um" over and over, you also don't want to be mute, which can—ironically—send a loud message about your leadership personal brand, e.g., that you believe you have nothing to offer.

I know you might be thinking, "Yes, but isn't it better to keep my mouth shut and be thought a fool than to open my mouth and remove all doubt?" I don't think so. If you're invited to a meeting, you're being paid to contribute to its success. Speak up if you have something to say. It's not only a great chance to share your ideas, but it's what you're *supposed* to do!

If you truly believe that you have nothing to contribute to a meeting, ask yourself what good it will do for your brand image to attend. If you still feel you *must* attend the meeting, sit at the back, not at the main table, and let the organizer of the meeting know that you are there only to observe. Keep in mind that if you decide to sit at the main table, you are expected to participate.

4. **Not directly answering the question you've been asked.** This may be a bit more about *what* you say, but this can be an important Sound Leadership Personal Brand Buster. Great self-branders answer direct questions... well, *directly*! A direct question is one that has a specific answer. For example, let's say that your Audience is considering two different campaigns developed by your ad agency for a new service that your consulting firm is preparing to launch. Your superior asks you directly: "Which one of these campaigns do you like the best?" Instead of answering directly, you say: "Well, I can see how Campaign #1 could potentially be more visible and noticeable, but I think Campaign #2 is actually more on strategy. On the other hand, Campaign #2 is less exciting. So, I guess there are benefits to both campaigns."

Did you answer the question? No! What are all the possible answers you could have said to this direct question? Either (a) "Campaign #1," or (b) "Campaign #2," or perhaps (c) "Neither!" No matter which answer you choose, the key is to *answer the question first*. Have an opinion and state it. Then, and only then, explain your choice, if necessary. Remember: You are being paid to have an opinion and share your point of view. Don't hesitate to do so directly.

Leadership Personal Brand Busters—Thoughts

1. **Believing you are the victim in situations at work.** What separates upbeat, successful people from those who aren't? I believe it's how they choose to interpret the events of their lives. As Winston Churchill said, "A pessimist sees the difficulty in every opportunity; an optimist sees the opportunity in every difficulty."

   If you constantly believe that people at work are "out to get you," you'll always be fearful and have a miserable work life. If you decide to look at life and your work as an *adventure*, with excitement about what might happen next, you'll be happier, more joyful, and ultimately, more peaceful. It's just the way it works. I can honestly say that *everything* negative that has ever happened to me has eventually taught me something amazing. It isn't a lot of "fun" to go through tough situations, but as author Denis Waitley put it, "There are no mistakes or failures, only lessons."

   We can choose to think of ourselves as victims, or we can choose to recognize every situation as an opportunity to improve ourselves. Smart leadership personal brand builders choose the latter! In fact, the happiest people are those who believe there are no such things as negative experiences—only opportunities to grow, learn, and advance along the road to self-mastery. Whenever something supposedly "bad" happens to me, I always sit back and ask myself: "What good will come out of this?" It may take a while, but eventually, something good *does* come from it.

   Here's a personal example: After a few years of working in the U.S., I reached a point when I had a strong desire to work overseas. I made it clear to my company several times that this was what I wanted, and finally—early one Monday morning—I was called into my boss's office where she shared the news: "You're moving to Prague!"

   I was ecstatic! I bought every book I could find about the Czech Republic and read all about it. What a gorgeous city Prague was!

Every book pointed to Prague as the best tourist destination in Central and Eastern Europe. I was thrilled.

But the *following* Monday morning, I was called into my boss's office again, and this time I heard: "Change of plans. You're moving to Warsaw, Poland instead." Now, no offense to Warsaw, but from the pictures I saw, it didn't look like Prague! I was devastated at the time—after all, for an entire week I had my head and heart set on moving to glorious Prague. It was an enormous blow to me. I did go ahead and agree to move to Poland, but I was admittedly not happy about it.

When I look back now on that decision, I have to laugh. Why? Because the decision to move to Warsaw was one of the best decisions I ever made in my life. You see, I moved there not long after the Berlin Wall had fallen, so Poland quickly became the powerhouse center of Central and Eastern European business development—the most rapidly growing economy in the region. Our company grew from 50 people when I arrived to more than 1,000 by the time I moved away just five years later. I was able to launch and grow a significant number of brands in a dynamic marketing environment that I would not have experienced in a smaller, less-growth-oriented country like the Czech Republic. All in all, it was an incredible time of career growth. And, on the personal front, I even met and married my husband while we were both expats living in Poland! It just goes to show you that what seems like something "bad" may actually turn out to be something better than good. In my experience, this has always been the case.

I encourage my coaching clients to avoid thinking of events as either negative or positive. I ask them to look at situations objectively, and celebrate the growth they have achieved as a result. In fact, right now, take a moment to think back on a time when you feel you grew the most. My guess is that it was the result of something that challenged you or that you considered "bad" at the time.

If you can adopt the habit of thinking of life and your career as an adventure and not "what's going to hurt me next," you'll stop worrying so much and enjoy yourself, expecting the best possible outcome. Once you do this, you'll be astonished by the change in your outlook. And the leadership personal brand you communicate will change for the better, too.

2. **Not accepting a task because you're afraid of failing.** Do you turn down opportunities—a challenging project or a great new job—because you're afraid you might fail? As I said in the Thoughts chapter, if you think you will fail, you probably will. How do you combat that annoying voice inside that says, "You'd better not try that. If you fail, you'll never get back to where you are now!"

Good leadership personal brand builders first take the time to understand the source of the fear. Often, the fear comes from the project seeming like a big hairy goal. When you see yourself at the foot of a mountain, and the goal you want to achieve is *waaaaaaay* at the top, it can feel insurmountable. But if you change your perspective and take just one small step at a time, the enormous task suddenly becomes doable.

Let's consider a city after it has just won the bid to host the Olympic Games. What do the most successful Olympics management teams do? They start early (they know their deadline), and they set an inspiring vision and goal. They understand their budget constraints, have a clear timeline with specific milestones, set out all the steps they will need to get to the endpoint, and then put the right resources in place to make it happen.

YOU™ can do this, too. The next time your Audience asks you to take on a seemingly gargantuan task, accept it! Simply cut it up into little pieces, and lay out a plan to tackle a small part of it every day or every week, as appropriate. You will learn, you will grow, and you will eventually get to the top of the mountain. And the view from up there will be great.

3. **Fearing feedback—both giving and receiving.** Despite the fact that most people don't particularly like feedback, it's one of the greatest gifts we can give or receive. Good leadership personal brand builders know that it's actually impossible to develop a leadership brand *unless* they receive open and honest feedback. You should ask for it regularly in order to make adjustments to how well you communicate your brand. Asking for feedback says to others that you're a professional, you're confident, and that

you want to improve. You don't have to make a big deal out of it. After a presentation or project is completed, simply say, "I'd love to have your thoughts about this project. What went well? What could have gone better?"

Learning to *give* meaningful feedback is also very powerful. You'll help others to improve and offer them the encouragement they need to excel. This is a skill that will definitely further any leadership personal brand.

4. **Believing "if it isn't 100% perfect, it isn't done."** This is the sign of a perfectionist. Another phrase perfectionists often think or say is, "Nobody else can do this as well as I can." Do you find yourself thinking these phrases? If so, you might be doing 20% more work than you need to get the job done.

    You've heard the old 80-for-20 rule, right? "If it's 80% done, then it's good enough." Nine times out of ten, this holds true, and people who don't believe that—the perfectionists who hang in there for that remaining 20%—are most likely spinning their wheels trying to finish the little bit that won't make a big difference in the long run. At the same time, the folks who *do* adhere to the 80-for-20 rule are finished with their original projects and moving on to the next ones. They're getting more accomplished and communicating a more productive and effective image to both management and clients.

    Be honest with yourself—will that extra 20% actually make a difference? If you really can't handle stopping at 80%, then aim to do 90%, and leave the remaining 10%. Once you see that the sky won't come tumbling down when that 10% doesn't get done, you'll start to become more comfortable with moving on to doing only 80%. It makes your life—and your perceived leadership personal brand—so much better. Remember that success is an achievable goal; perfection is not.

Which Busters Do YOU™ Need to Bust?

On the next page is a quiz to help you better understand how YOU™ do on a regular basis with our top 20 most common Leadership Personal Brand Busters. If you think you commit a particular Buster at least

50% of the time or more, mark it "yes." If you think you commit that particular Buster less than 50% of the time, mark it "no."

At the end of the quiz is a key to score your answers. When you're finished, you'll have a clear idea of how much work you need to do to keep from damaging your leadership personal brand. But even if your score is a bit disappointing, take heart. As author F. Wikzek said, "If you don't make mistakes, you're not working on hard enough problems. And *that's* a big mistake."

No matter your score, with this book and the *Master the Brand Called YOU™* leadership personal branding system, you have a roadmap for getting your leadership personal brand in shape like never before. Don't dwell on the past. Think in terms of what you will do from this moment on to make things better. After each Buster, jot down Action steps that you will take to bust that particular Buster. What will you do to make sure you don't commit each Buster again?

Do You Occasionally Commit These Leadership Personal Brand Busters?

		Actions

Yes	No		Action Steps
☐	☐	1. Offering an inappropriate handshake.	
☐	☐	2. Asking permission to make decisions within your scope of responsibility.	
☐	☐	3. Working on less important, easier tasks before tackling the tough ones.	
☐	☐	4. Working non-stop without taking a break.	

Reactions

Yes No   <u>Action Steps</u>

☐ ☐ 5. Taking yourself and the situation too seriously.

☐ ☐ 6. Acting like you understand something when you really don't.

☐ ☐ 7. Consistently giving up previously scheduled personal plans for work.

☐ ☐ 8. "Delegating back up" when you can't complete an assigned task.

Look

Yes No   <u>Action Steps</u>

☐ ☐ 9. Underestimating the impact of proper eye contact.

☐ ☐ 10. Dressing inappropriately for the situation.

☐ ☐ 11. Thinking that "Look" only means aspects of your person or your office.

☐ ☐ 12. Ignoring the importance of breath and body odor as part of your "Look."

Sound

<u>Yes</u> <u>No</u>   <u>Action Steps</u>

☐ ☐ 13. Ignoring the importance of
          silence as a powerful Sound.

☐ ☐ 14. Feeling the need to fill silence
          with "ums."

☐ ☐ 15. Not speaking up at a meeting
          you've been invited to attend.

☐ ☐ 16. Not directly answering the
          question you've been asked.

Thoughts

<u>Yes</u> <u>No</u>   <u>Action Steps</u>

☐ ☐ 17. Believing you are the victim in
          situations at work.

☐ ☐ 18. Not accepting a task because
          you're afraid of failing.

☐ ☐ 19. Fearing feedback—both giving
          and receiving.

☐ ☐ 20. Believing "if it isn't 100% perfect,
          it isn't done."

Scoring Your Leadership Personal Brand Busters Quiz

Count the number of times you responded "yes," and compare your final number against this Leadership Personal Brand Busters scorecard:

Leadership Personal Brand Busters Scorecard

If the number of "yes" responses you gave is ...

0 to 5   You're obviously a strong leadership personal brand builder with excellent self-leadership. Keep up the good work, and don't stop until you have zero "yes" responses.

6 to 10   Choose one or two areas you think could make the biggest difference in your leadership personal brand image, and set up a plan to focus on changing those self-leadership behaviors in the next couple of months.

11 to 20   The good news is: You've uncovered a number of opportunities to strengthen your leadership personal brand. Identify three specific Busters you want to focus on during the next six months. Then, find a mentor or coach to provide feedback and encouragement along the way as you work on changing your leadership personal brand image. It's never too late to change your brand. Bravo to you for taking the first step!

Whatever your score on the quiz, I tip my hat to you and to the work you've done toward making your desired leadership personal brand a reality. Now, let's make sure you take the steps necessary to guarantee you'll be successful at building your brand long term.

The Proven Pathway to Branding YOU™

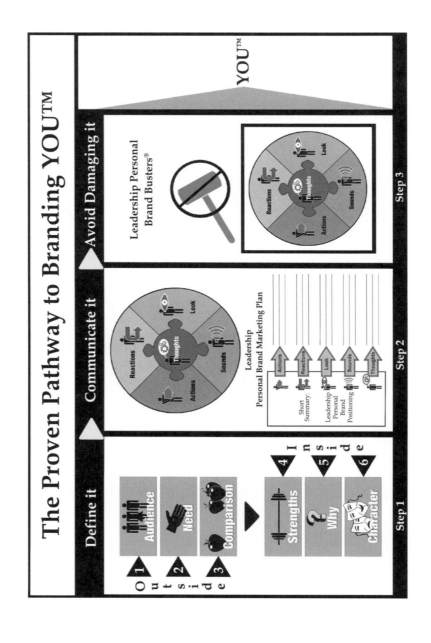

20

Assuring Long-Term Success

I do not think that there is any other quality so essential to success of any kind as the quality of perseverance. It overcomes almost everything, even nature.

— John D. Rockefeller, U.S. industrialist and philanthropist

As we near the end of this journey, it's a good idea to sit back and reflect on just how far you've come in developing your own unique leadership personal brand called YOU™. Together, we have applied each step of this system to help you discover your own leadership personal brand. We have:

✓ Looked at what leadership personal branding is and what impact it can have on your workplace, career, compensation, promotion opportunities, recognition, etc.

✓ Defined the six core elements that make up your leadership personal brand—Audience, Need, Comparison, Unique Strengths, Reasons Why, and Brand Character—and pulled these elements together to create your distinctive and unique Leadership Personal Brand Positioning Statement.

✓ Explored how to communicate your leadership personal brand through the five self-leadership activities you do every day that most impact your brand: your Actions, Reactions, Look, Sound, and Thoughts.

✓ Developed a Leadership Personal Brand Marketing Plan uniquely for YOU™, outlining what specific Actions, Reactions, Look, Sound, and Thoughts you will adopt to make sure you communicate your brand accurately and consistently.

✓ Reviewed how to avoid damaging your leadership personal brand by watching out for several key Leadership Personal Brand Busters®—both the 20 common ones from our quiz, along with specific ones from your own private list.

Along the way, you've asked yourself and others some powerful questions. You've had the chance to look at your current leadership personal brand from an objective viewpoint. You've been able to craft a vision of what you want your desired brand to be. Bottom line: You've become a great leadership personal brand builder, working toward building your brand with an Audience focus. Well done!

Of course, like any good marketer with a strong strategy, it isn't enough to simply have a plan. You have to follow through and stick to that plan consistently, day in and day out.

Make Success a Done Deal

How do you make sure this path you've laid out toward your desired leadership personal brand—which is paved with good intentions— doesn't turn into a dead end? Here are a few suggestions to keep you on track:

- Be confident. In a study conducted at the University of Washington, they found that participants who simply had more confidence in themselves were more likely to keep their New Year's resolutions. In other words, the participants who *believed* they could achieve their goals actually *did* achieve them.

- Recognize that building your brand is a process, not a one-time effort. You're trying to create new habits and embrace new behaviors, so be both persistent and patient. In that same

University of Washington study, only 40% of the people who successfully achieved their top New Year's resolution did so on their first attempt. The rest tried several times, and 17% finally succeeded after more than six tries. So, if you make a mistake or two, don't beat yourself up. Persistence will eventually pay off.

- Stay committed to the vision of your leadership personal brand. Develop a visual symbol that stands for your brand image. Keep it somewhere near you as a reminder. You could put it in your pocket or your wallet on the same paper as your leadership personal brand summary so that you see or feel it every time you reach in to pull out some money. It's a great way to remember your leadership personal brand goals.

- First thing each week, set specific, measurable Actions, Reactions, Look, Sound, or Thoughts goals to move you closer to achieving your overall desired leadership personal brand. Reward yourself at the end of the week for having achieved them.

- Are you feeling a bit overwhelmed because you want to change quite a few activities in your Leadership Personal Brand Marketing Plan? If so, take baby steps. This month, just focus on one or two parts of your Marketing Plan. Which one or two activities could make the biggest difference? Start there. When you are ready, you can always focus on more activities later.

- When you are faced with a tough challenge that makes you react in a way that's inconsistent with your desired leadership personal brand, review your list of coping strategies. Remind yourself of the "big picture," crawl out of the details of the situation, and try to see what's going on objectively. Imagine you're 30,000 feet in the air with a bird's-eye viewpoint.

- Find a trusted confidante at work to become your "leadership personal brand accountability buddy." You can help each other stay on track with your respective Leadership Personal Brand Marketing Plans and support each other along the way. Another option is to consider hiring a coach or finding a mentor, if possible, to hold you accountable for your goals and to help give you an objective perspective.

- Keep track of your progress. Monitor yourself, make note of your successes, and regularly reward yourself for meeting your objectives.

How Will You Know When You've Reached Your Desired Leadership Personal Brand?

You will know you've reached your desired leadership personal brand *when your Audience tells you so!* Remember: Your leadership personal brand is the way you want others to perceive, think, and feel about you. That means you'll need to check back once in a while so that you know when those "others" truly perceive, think, and feel about YOU™ the way you want.

To make sure you are staying on track and to determine how well you are doing in your leadership personal branding efforts, perform regular self-checks. Review the chapters outlining the six leadership personal brand positioning elements as well as the key questions to ask yourself and your Audience.

For example:

Audience and Need. These may not have changed, but it's a good idea to double-check—particularly in terms of Needs—to make sure no new Audience Needs have surfaced.

Comparison. Have any new options entered your Comparison List?

Unique Strengths. Are you exhibiting your Unique Strengths, and is your Audience noticing them?

Reasons Why. Does your Audience recognize your Reasons Why as solid enough reasons to believe you can deliver your Unique Strengths?

Leadership Personal Brand Character. Is your leadership personal Brand Character coming through, and is your Audience perceiving, thinking, and feeling about you in this way?

Set milestones for yourself, and stay disciplined about checking in with your Audience every eight weeks … three months … six months.

Evolve Your Leadership Personal Brand

As human beings, we aren't static, nor are we intended to be. Your leadership personal brand will grow and evolve over time, just as corporate brands evolve. Remember when Apple only stood for the Macintosh computer? Now, Apple stands for much, much more. It has evolved its brand considerably in the past few years and is now an active brand evolver. You might also remember brands like Kodak, which hung its hat on film and took too long to respond to the growing digital camera trend. That's a brand that didn't evolve as quickly as it should have.

Just like these corporate brands, you have to evolve your own brand to fit with the changes that are happening around you. Watch for how the elements of your leadership personal brand might need to change and how those changes will impact your leadership personal brand development and evolution:

- Maybe you change jobs, your boss is replaced, or you decide to take on a new type of internal customer. All of these events will impact the Audience part of your leadership personal brand.

- If your Audience changes, you must redefine your new Audience's *Needs*. Sometimes, your Audience itself doesn't change, but circumstances cause your existing Audience's Needs to change. That means you must revise your leadership personal brand as a result. Never forget how critical your Audience's Needs are to defining YOU™!

- Is your company moving toward outsourcing a part of your job, or are there new hires that need to be added to your Comparison List? Stay aware of the impact these changes can have on your brand.

- As you evolve your Unique Strengths, what additional opportunities do they open up for you? Could your new Unique Strengths lead you to a promotion or to greater responsibility? Stay aware of these possibilities, and take advantage of them.

- As you beef up your Reasons Why, notice again what new opportunities may present themselves to you. Don't forget to note the Reasons Why of your new Comparison List additions, too. Are your previously defined Reasons Why still strong enough, or have changes at work made it necessary for you to develop even stronger ones?

- Are you being true to your leadership personal Brand Character? Typically, your Character doesn't change all that much over time—usually only as a result of something major that causes a substantial life change. Has anything like this happened to you that would influence the way others perceive your Brand Character? If so, what are the implications on your overall brand?

My Personal Note to YOU™

What a trip it has been to ride along with you on this road toward your leadership personal brand—YOU™! I hope to hear from you about your brand successes, challenges, and questions as you craft your Leadership Personal Brand Positioning Statement and put your Leadership Personal Brand Marketing Plan into action. Please write me at Brenda@BrendaBence.com. I look forward to hearing how your brand is coming along.

Congratulations on taking control of your career success by learning to craft and communicate your own unique brand at work. Happy branding to YOU™! I wish you a lifetime of fulfillment and great achievements.

Appendix

Self-Awareness Assessments

Assessment.com

www.assessment.com

MAPP is a personal assessment that takes about 15 minutes to complete. MAPP identifies your strengths and your true motivations toward work. You can receive a free report, and if you like what you see, you can choose to purchase a full report. There are four options from free to packages ranging from $89.95 to $149.95 (for the full executive package). You can view report options and choose the best one for you.

Careering Ahead

www.careeringahead.com.au

Free. Out of Australia, this is a secured, online psychometric test. Self-described as a "simple and user-friendly process to make taking a psychometric test an enjoyable experience," the firm recommends you take it in a quiet place and make sure you are undisturbed during this process. The test is thorough and has about 4oo questions.

Keirsey

www.keirsey.com

Retail Price: $19.95. Check out the Career Temperament Report, which can help you to pinpoint your innate strengths.

Similarminds

www.similarminds.com

Free. Provides various tests such as 16 Type Jung Personality Tests, Personality Disorder Test, Compatibility Test, Career Test, Personality Test, Intelligence Test, etc. After you take a test, it provides instant feedback, usually in the form of a brief paragraph.

Strengths Finder
www.strengthsfinder.com

After you purchase the book, *Now, Discover Your Strengths,* there is a code inside which allows you to access the StrengthsFinder online.

Gallup introduced the first version of its online assessment, StrengthsFinder, in the 2001 management book, *Now, Discover Your Strengths*. In StrengthsFinder 2.0, Gallup unveils the new and improved version of its popular assessment, Language of 34 Themes, and much more. You can read the book in one sitting, but they say "you'll use it as a reference for decades." These highly customized Strengths Insights will help you understand how each of your top five themes plays out in your life on a much more personal and professional level. The Strengths Insights describe what makes you stand out when compared to the millions of people that Gallup has studied.

This information, while verified and correct at the time of printing, is subject to change at any time. Please contact each provider directly to inquire about current tests and pricing. Thank you!

About the Author

Brenda S. Bence understands the challenges of working in today's global environment. She is Founder and President of BDA (Brand Development Associates) Int'l Ltd., a firm with offices in both the U.S. and Asia that specializes in helping companies and individual clients around the world build successful, growth-oriented corporate and personal brands. As an international speaker, trainer, and executive coach, she has coached more than 700 senior leaders from many of the world's largest and most recognized companies, helping them define and communicate their corporate and leadership personal brands.

Brenda earned an MBA from Harvard Business School and spent a large part of her career as an executive with Procter & Gamble and Bristol-Myers Squibb. There, she was responsible for marketing mega-brands like Pantene, Vidal Sassoon, Head & Shoulders, and Enfamil across four continents and almost 50 countries.

Besides her individual and leadership-team coaching services, Brenda is also an in-demand speaker at conferences, conventions, and company meetings across Southeast Asia, Greater China, the U.S./ North America, Western & Eastern Europe, the Indian Subcontinent, Australia/New Zealand, and Africa. She has presented her dynamic programs for such clients as Abbott, Bank of America Merrill Lynch, Boston Consulting Group, Credit Suisse, Danone, Deloitte, General Electric, KFC, Kraft, Lilly, Mattel, Microsoft, Pizza Hut, Royal Bank of Scotland (RBS), Radisson Hotels, Sheraton Hotels, Standard Chartered Bank, and UBS AG.

Leadership Excellence's annual top 500 ranking has recognized Brenda's proprietary leadership development program as one of the top 25 in the world for Independent Trainers & Coaches.

Brenda is also the author of several books that have collectively won 24 national and international book awards, and her magazine and newspaper columns related to branding, leadership, and executive coaching have been published in over 400 media outlets. These include

Investor's Business Daily, Affluent, The Financial Times, The Los Angeles Times, Entrepreneur, Kiplinger's Personal Finance, Reader's Digest, Cosmopolitan, and *The Wall Street Journal's SmartMoney.*

A popular guest on television and radio, Brenda also sits on boards of both public and private companies, as well as not-for-profit organizations. She has traveled to more than 80 countries, is an avid Mahjong player, and enjoys studying foreign languages.

Visit www.BrendaBence.com or write Brenda@BrendaBence.com for more information.

Acknowledgments

There's nothing to writing. All you do is sit down at a typewriter and open a vein.
— Walter Wellesley "Red" Smith

Writing a book is indeed akin to "opening a vein"—it's truly a labor of love. And, as with any book, it is never just one person who makes it happen. I'm grateful to so many who have offered their incredible talents to turn this book from a Thought into reality. Heartfelt thanks go to:

My leadership personal branding coaching clients, who have allowed me to accompany them on their journeys of self-branding discovery.

Mike Maloney and Richard Czierniawski, two incredible marketing minds, with whom I have enjoyed a wonderful, productive business relationship over the years. Thanks for your ongoing support and personal friendship.

My outstanding team of coaches and experts from all around the world:

- U.S: Melanie Votaw, a truly fantastic editor
- Australia: Jay Cotton for his great system design, quick work, and can-do attitude
- India: Eric Myhr for excellent interior design and typesetting services
- U.S: Graham Dixhorn of Write to Your Market for book cover text

Besides those who actually worked "on" the book, there were people who tirelessly cheered me on. My sincere gratitude goes to:

Daniel, for the non-stop support and laughter you bring to me every single day ... I couldn't imagine a better partner in life.

Mom, for teaching me to laugh from the get-go ... for almond balls at year-end, apple butter surprises, and potato salad on the 4th of July.

Kathie Uhrmacher, Brett Bence, and Craig Bence, siblings & LLC partners extraordinaire — how fortunate we are to have each other!

Danielle Johnston, my supportive and talented soul sister of four decades, for your uncanny ability to make me laugh... anytime, anywhere.

The entire team at BDA International for keeping the machine well-oiled and functioning while I was in the throes of writing.

Friends, associates, and business colleagues to whom I have had to say "no" during this writing time when I really wanted to say "yes." Please know that my spirit was with you even though my body was at the computer, typing away ....

To My Team, always-present, ever-guiding.

Services Provided by Brenda Bence

Speaking Engagements

Brenda is in demand as a conference, convention, and corporate speaker, not only for her unique approach to corporate and personal branding, marketing, and leadership development, but also for her warm, dynamic, and engaging style. Her popular one- to two-hour keynote addresses "enter-train" your group as she shares enlightening and humorous stories from her years as a corporate brander and Certified Executive Coach. Her practical, no-nonsense approach provides every participant in the room with strategies that they can put into action the minute they walk out of the door. One of only a fraction of speakers worldwide who have earned the Certified Speaking Professional designation by the National Speakers Association, Brenda is also a member of the Global Speakers Federation and Asia Professional Speakers. Throughout her career, she has shared her powerful presentations with tens of thousands, and in the process, she has guided audiences around the world to greater career success and fulfillment.

Executive Coaching

Brenda has coached more than 700 senior leaders from over 60 nationalities across six continents and 70 different industries. She offers in-person, video, and telephone coaching to C-Suite Executives, Senior Leaders, Business Owners, and Board Members located anywhere in the world. With 20 years of both internal and external coaching experience, Brenda will give you perspective and encouragement—much like having a partner "running alongside you" at work—as you put your Leadership Brand into action. Just as a personal trainer helps you craft a plan to reach pre-defined fitness goals and then stretches you to reach those goals, Brenda works with you to think *bigger* and helps you break down objectives into actionable steps that allow you to build the brand you want to have. Brenda is a Certified Coach with the International Coach Federation and with Results™ Coaching Systems (Australia), and she is a member of the Asia Pacific Alliance of Coaches.

Corporate Training

Brenda's interactive corporate training programs will change the way you and your team look at branding, marketing, and leadership development. Customized for the specific needs of your company, Brenda can focus on one or more of her areas of expertise in both in-person or online interactive workshops. Leveraging her extensive corporate experience, she will show you and your team how to build powerhouse personal and corporate brands that can dramatically improve your company's bottom line. Step by step, she can walk your leadership team and employees through her breakthrough, practical leadership personal branding system, showing them how to turn "you" into "YOU™" for better on-the-job achievement and visibility. Combining these unique qualifications, she will demonstrate to your team how the success of your company's brand largely depends on the success of each of their individual personal brands. With Brenda's workshops, one thing is guaranteed: Participants don't just sit on the sidelines and watch. Each attendee is highly involved in the learning process, and your group will apply their new skills to exercises that represent the actual day-to-day challenges they encounter at work.

Visit www.BrendaBence.com or write Brenda@BrendaBence.com for more information.